Cambridge English

EXAM BOOSTER

WITH ANSWER KEY

FOR KEY AND KEY FOR SCHOOLS

Photocopiable exam resources for teachers

Caroline Chapman and Susan White

Cambridge University Press
www.cambridge.org/elt

Cambridge English Language Assessment
www.cambridgeenglish.org

Information on this title: www.cambridge.org/9781316648452

© Cambridge University Press and UCLES 2017

This publication is in copyright. Subject to statutory exception and to the provisions of relevant collective licensing agreements, no reproduction of any part may take place without the written permission of Cambridge University Press.

20 19 18 17 16 15 14 13 12 11 10 9 8 7 6 5 4 3 2 1

Printed in Spain by GraphyCems

A catalogue record for this publication is available from the British Library

ISBN 978-1-316-64845-2

Additional resources for this publication at www.cambridge.org/keybooster

Cambridge University Press has no responsibility for the persistence or accuracy of URLs for external or third-party internet websites referred to in this publication, and does not guarantee that any content on such websites is, or will remain, accurate or appropriate. Information regarding prices, travel timetables, and other factual information given in this work is correct at the time of first printing but Cambridge University Press does not guarantee the accuracy of such information thereafter.

CONTENTS

MAP OF THE BOOK

Paper 1: Reading and Writing 1 hour 10 minutes	Worksheet 1	Worksheet 2	Worksheet 3
Reading and Writing Part 1 p12 Matching 5 questions 5 marks	**Daily life** Present simple and adverbs of frequency Daily routine questions	**Places and buildings** Places vocabulary Asking for and giving information	**Services** Services vocabulary Understanding signs and notices
Reading and Writing Part 2 p18 3-option multiple choice 5 questions 5 marks	**Shopping** Shopping vocabulary Costs and amounts	**Food and drink** Food and drink vocabulary Ordering in a restaurant	**House and home** Adjectives Basic furniture and prepositions
Reading and Writing Part 3 p24 3-option multiple choice AND matching 10 questions 10 marks	**Social interaction** Questions Responding to invitations	**Feelings, opinions and experiences** Present perfect + *just, yet, already, never, ever, for* and *since*	**Hobbies and leisure** Hobbies vocabulary Arranging a social activity
Reading and Writing Part 4 p30 3-option multiple choice OR Right/Wrong/Doesn't say 7 questions 7 marks	**The natural world** Landscape vocabulary Expressing agreement and disagreement	**Education and study** School subjects vocabulary Past simple and past events	**Travel and holidays** Travel vocabulary Directions
Reading and Writing Part 5 p36 3-option multiple choice cloze 8 questions 8 marks	**Sports and games** *go, play* and *do* Past simple and past continuous	**Entertainment and media** Music vocabulary Suggesting, accepting and refusing	**Transport** Comparatives and superlatives Making predictions
Reading and Writing Part 6 p42 Spelling 5 questions 5 marks	**The weather** Letters and pronunciation Talking about the weather	**Clothes** Things to wear Pronouns	**People** Describing people Adjectives describing people
Reading and Writing Part 7 p48 Open cloze 10 questions 10 marks	**Daily life** Present simple and daily routine Email describing typical day	**Social interaction** Modals: possibility, ability and permission Present continuous and time expressions	**Travel and holidays** Past simple: irregular verbs Talking about future plans
Reading and Writing Part 8 p54 Information transfer 5 questions 5 marks	**Hobbies and leisure** Understanding short messages Expressing preferences	**Sport and activities** Sports vocabulary Completing a form with personal details	**Food and drink** Food groups Food preparation verbs
Reading and Writing Part 9 p60 Guided writing 1 question 5 marks	**Health and exercise** Mixed tenses Writing an email	**Personal identification** Family vocabulary Giving personal information	**Entertainment and media** Entertainment vocabulary Using punctuation

Paper 2: Listening About 30 minutes	Worksheet 1	Worksheet 2	Worksheet 3
Listening Part 1 p66 3-option multiple choice 5 questions 5 marks	**Services and places** Times, days and dates Places in town vocabulary	**Shopping and numbers** Numbers Shopping vocabulary	**Education and study** Present, future and past actions Daily routine
Listening Part 2 p72 Matching 5 questions 5 marks	**Food and drink** *this, that, these* and *those* Countable and uncountable	**Hobbies and shopping** Offers and requests Likes and preferences	**Countries and sports** Languages and nationalities Suggestions and responding
Listening Part 3 p78 3-option multiple choice 5 questions 5 marks	**Leisure time** Giving information about days, dates, times and prices Free time vocabulary	**Social media and technology** Digital world vocabulary Present and past simple passive	**Travel and holidays** Documents and texts vocabulary Talking about future plans
Listening Part 4 p84 Gap-fill 5 questions 5 marks	**Making plans** Time vocabulary and prepositions of time *Going to* and *will*	**Health, medicine and exercise** Parts of the body vocabulary Modals of advice	**Dates and services** Dates, months and events Giving the time, day or date
Listening Part 5 p90 Gap-fill 5 questions 5 marks	**House and home** Home vocabulary Word order in questions	**Entertainment and media** Taking down and giving phone numbers Imperatives	**Education and study** Expressing rules Modals of obligation

Paper 3: Speaking 8–10 minutes	Worksheet 1	Worksheet 2	Worksheet 3
Speaking Part 1 p96 Examiner asks questions 5–6 minutes	**Personal identification** Giving information about yourself Family vocabulary	**Daily life** Time expressions Word order and adverbs of frequency	**Places and buildings** Places in town vocabulary Talking about places you go to
Speaking Part 2 p102 Candidates exchange information 3-4 minutes	**Hobbies and leisure** Giving information about routines Seasons and months	**Sport** Action verbs Present simple questions	**Holidays and travel** Transport vocabulary Mixed tenses

Think about it p108

Key topic lists p116

Answer key p125

Go to http://www.cambridgeenglish.org/exams/general-english-and-for-schools/ for useful information about preparing for the *Cambridge English: Key* and *Key for Schools* exams.

HOW TO USE THE EXAM BOOSTER

Welcome to the Cambridge English

What is the Exam Booster?

The Exam Booster provides focused exam practice of all parts of the *Cambridge English: Key* and *Cambridge English: Key for Schools* exam. Prepare your students for the exam, ensuring they gain the confidence, skills and knowledge they need for exam day.

How can I use it?

• Pick and choose the areas you want to practise at any time
• Use alongside a coursebook or on its own; in class or for homework
• Photocopy worksheets for ease of use
• Use it flexibly to best support your students

How is it structured?

The Exam Booster contains 16 sections which follow the order of the exam: Reading and Writing Parts 1–9, Listening Parts 1–5 and finally Speaking Parts 1 and 2.

Check exam paper, exam part and worksheet number at the top of each section.

Find exam tasks easily. There are **three** worksheets for **each** exam part.

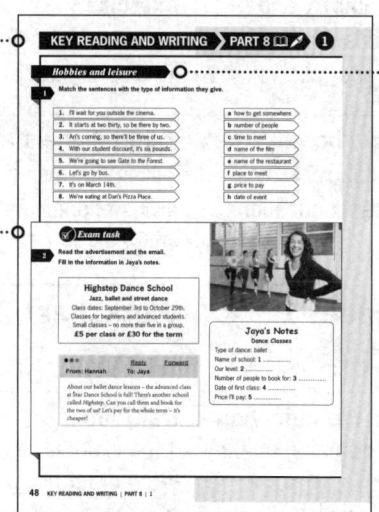

Cover a variety of topics from the exam. Topics are suitable for both *Cambridge English: Key* and *Cambridge English: Key for Schools* preparation.

Go to www.cambridge.org/keybooster to download the audio to your computer or device.

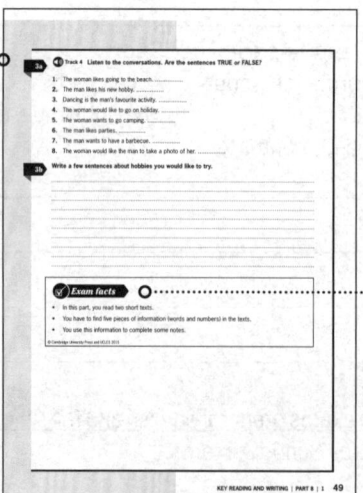

Exam facts offer clear, concise information about the exercise type and number of questions.

What other features are there?

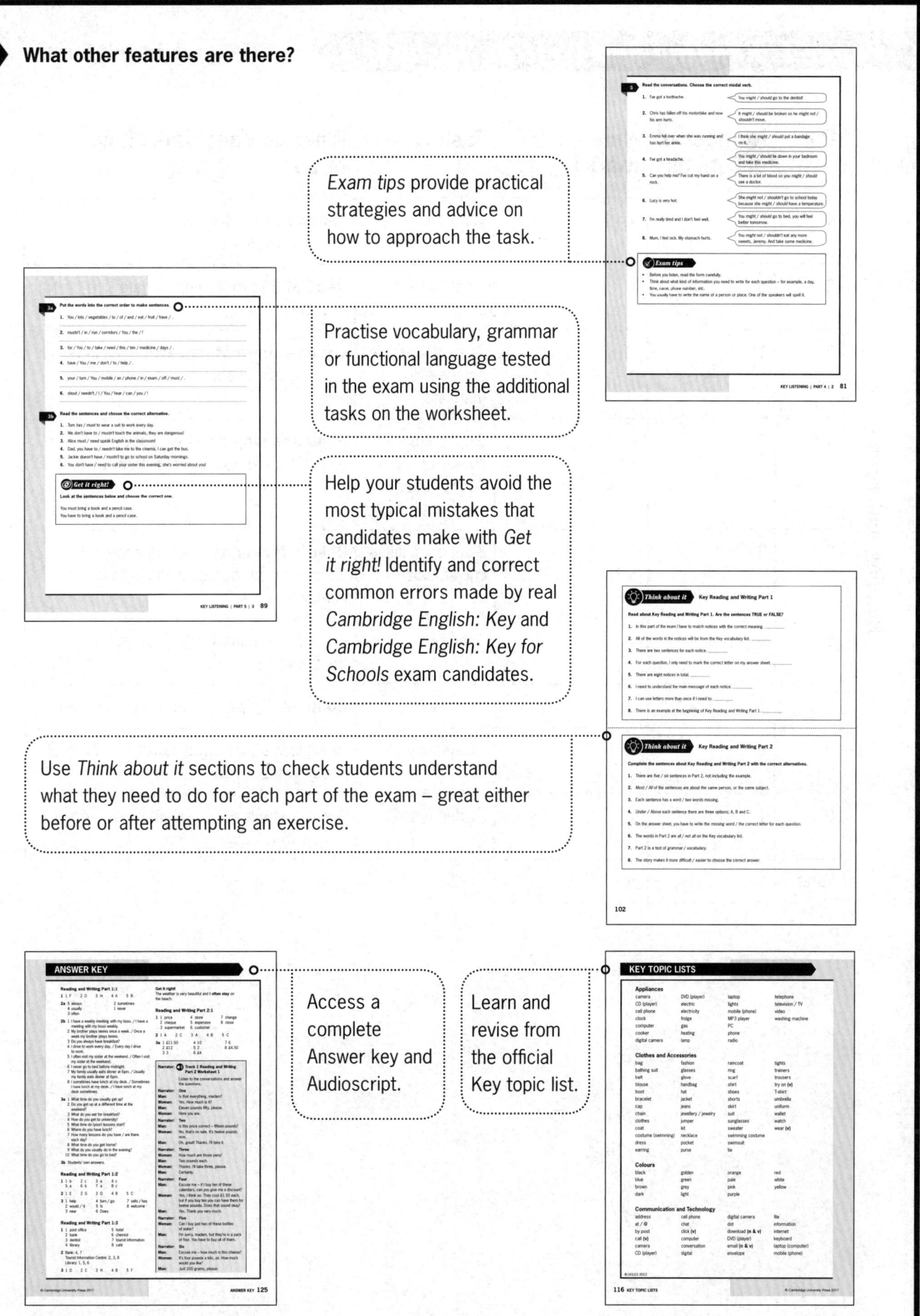

Exam tips provide practical strategies and advice on how to approach the task.

Practise vocabulary, grammar or functional language tested in the exam using the additional tasks on the worksheet.

Help your students avoid the most typical mistakes that candidates make with *Get it right!* Identify and correct common errors made by real *Cambridge English: Key* and *Cambridge English: Key for Schools* exam candidates.

Use *Think about it* sections to check students understand what they need to do for each part of the exam – great either before or after attempting an exercise.

Access a complete Answer key and Audioscript.

Learn and revise from the official Key topic list.

Paper 1: Reading and Writing Tasks 📖   1 hour 10 mins

Reading and Writing

Part	Number of questions	Number of marks	Task type	What do candidates have to do?
1	5	5	Matching	**Match five sentences** to eight real-world notices.
2	5	5	3-option multiple choice	**Read and identify** appropriate vocabulary.
3	10	10	3-option multiple choice AND matching	**Choose appropriate responses** in verbal exchanges and continuous dialogue.
4	7	7	3-option multiple choice or Right/ Wrong/Doesn't say questions	**Read one long or three short texts** for detailed understanding and main idea(s).
5	8	8	3-option multiple choice cloze	**Read a factual text** and choose the correct grammatical items to complete gaps.
6	5	5	Spelling	**Identify and spell** individual words from definitions.
7	10	10	Open cloze	**Complete gaps in text** using one word.
8	5	5	Information transfer	**Read two short input texts** and complete gaps in output text.
9	1	5	Guided writing	**Write a short note, email or postcard** of 25–35 words.
Total	56	60		

Paper 2: Listening tasks 🔊

about 30 mins
(including 8 minutes to transfer answers)

Part	Number of questions	Number of marks	Task type	What do candidates have to do?
1	5	5	3-option multiple choice	**Identify key information in five short dialogues** and choose the correct visual.
2	5	5	Matching	**Listen to a dialogue** for key information and match five items.
3	5	5	3-option multiple choice	**Listen to a dialogue** for key information and answer five 3-option questions.
4	5	5	Gap-fill	**Listen to a dialogue** and complete gaps in a page of notes.
5	5	5	Gap-fill	**Listen to a monologue** and complete gaps in a page of notes.
Total	25	25		

(Listening)

Paper 3: Speaking tasks 💬

8–10 mins

Part	Timing	Interaction	Task type	What do candidates have to do?
1	5–6 minutes	Examiner ↓ Candidate	Examiner asks questions to each candidate in turn	**Respond to questions**, giving factual or personal information.
2	3–4 minutes	Candidate ↑↓ Candidate	Information exchange	**Candidates ask and answer questions** about factual, non-personal information using prompt material.
	Total	25 marks		

(Speaking)

Cambridge English

The Cambridge English Scale explained

A guide to converting *Cambridge English: Key* and *Key for Schools* practice test scores to Cambridge English Scale scores

Cambridge English: Key and *Key for Schools* are now reporting results on the Cambridge English Scale. For these exams, candidates receive an individual score for each of the three papers - Reading and Writing, Listening and Speaking. In the live exams, the Reading and Writing paper tests two skills, so the score is doubled. The overall score is calculated by adding all of the individual scores together and dividing by four (and then rounding to the nearest whole number). A candidate's grade and CEFR level are based on their performance across the whole test, and there is no requirement to achieve a minimum score in each paper.

The following tables can be used as guidance to help you convert practice test scores to Cambridge English Scale scores.

Please note that these only apply when using official Cambridge practice tests.

The conversion tables are intended to help you provide an indication of your students' readiness to take the relevant exam. The scores you provide may not always reflect the results the students may achieve in a Cambridge English live exam. They should not be used to try to predict precise scores in the live exam, but can be a useful diagnostic tool, indicating areas of relative strength and weakness.

The scores needed on any given test to achieve the scores on the Cambridge English Scale shown in the tables below will vary due to a number of factors, so borderline scores need to be reviewed carefully. The borderline is approximately three Cambridge English scale score points above and below the score needed to achieve the level, e.g. 117-123 for Level A2. Students who achieve only slightly higher than the Cambridge English Scale score for a given level on a practice test may not achieve that level in the live exam, and we recommend that they continue working to improve so that they reach the desired level.

CAMBRIDGE ENGLISH
Language Assessment
Part of the University of Cambridge

Converting *Cambridge English: Key* and *Key for Schools*
practice test scores to Cambridge English Scale scores

Cambridge English
Key

Cambridge English
Key
for Schools

Reading and Writing

The Reading and Writing paper consists of 9 parts. Correct answers in Parts 1–8 are worth 1 mark each and Part 9 is worth 5 marks. There are 60 possible marks in the Reading and Writing paper.

Practice test score	Cambridge English Scale score	CEFR Level
55	140	Level B1
40	120	Level A2
25	100	Level A1
13	82*	-

*minimum score reported for *Key*

Listening

Correct answers in the Listening paper are worth 1 mark each. There are 25 possible marks in the Listening paper.

Practice test score	Cambridge English Scale score	CEFR Level
23	140	Level B1
17	120	Level A2
11	100	Level A1
6	82*	-

*minimum score reported for *Key*

Speaking

Candidates take the test in pairs, but are assessed on their individual performance by trained examiners certificated to examine at the level. Candidate speaking performances are assessed using scales which are linked to the Common European Framework of Reference. The assessor gives 0–5 marks for each of the following criteria: Grammar and Vocabulary; Pronunciation; and Interactive Communication. Marks for each of these criteria are doubled. The interlocutor gives a mark of 0–5 for Global Achievement. This mark is then multiplied by three. Examiners may award half marks. Marks for all criteria are then combined, meaning there are 45 marks available in the Speaking test.

Practice test score	Cambridge English Scale score	CEFR Level
41	140	Level B1
27	120	Level A2
18	100	Level A1
10	82*	-

*minimum score reported for *Key*

Daily life

☑ Exam task

1 Which notice (A–H) says this (1–5)? For questions (1–5), write the correct answer.

1. You can have this meal at any time.

2. You can only leave your car here in the afternoon or evening.

3. This place is cheaper in the evening.

4. There is someone here to help all day and night.

5. You must get to this place early.

A | *Travel information office* <u>Open 24 hours</u>

B | Please arrive at least **10 minutes before** the time of your appointment.

C | Staff restaurant *Sorry – we've closed early this afternoon.* **Open normal time tomorrow.**

D | <u>NO PARKING</u> between midnight and midday.

E | **Drive-through restaurant** *Open Thursday, Friday and Saturday 8 pm to midnight*

F | **CAFÉ** Our popular breakfasts are available all day at excellent prices!

G | **SHORT-STAY CAR PARK** £2.50 for two hours

H | All drinks half-price **AFTER 5 PM.**

2a Put the adverbs in the box in the correct order, from the most frequent (5) to the least frequent (1).

sometimes .... never .... often ....
always .... usually ....

2b Rewrite the sentences with the words or expressions in brackets in the correct place.

1. I have a meeting with my boss. (weekly)

....

2. My brother plays tennis. (once a week)

....

3. Do you have breakfast? (always)

....

4. I drive to work. (every day)

....

5. I visit my sister at the weekend. (often)

....

6. I go to bed before midnight. (never)

....

7. My family eat dinner at 6 pm. (usually)

....

8. I have lunch at my desk. (sometimes)

....

3a **Write the questions.**

1. time | usually | get up? ....
2. get up | different | time | at the weekend? ....
3. what | eat | for breakfast? ....
4. how | get | university? ....
5. time | lessons | start? ....
6. where | have | lunch? ....
7. how many | lessons | each day? ....
8. time | get | home? ....
9. what | usually | do | evening? ....
10. time | go | bed? ....

3b **Write your answers to five questions from Activity 3a. Use adverbs of frequency.**

1. ....
2. ....
3. ....
4. ....
5. ....

☑ **Exam facts**

- In this part, you read seven short texts. These are usually signs or notices.
- There are also five sentences.
- For each sentence, you have to choose the text that means the same thing.
- There are three texts that you don't need.

© Cambridge University Press and UCLES 2015

Places and buildings

1 **Read the descriptions. Choose the correct answer, a, b or c.**

1. You go here if you want to catch a plane.
   a station   **b** airport   **c** motorway
2. People go here to watch sports such as football.
   a roundabout   **b** theatre   **c** stadium
3. You can park your car in one of these.
   a garage   **b** lift   **c** underground
4. Businessmen and businesswomen work at desks in this place.
   a elevator   **b** pharmacy   **c** office
5. Parents take their children here so they can have fun.
   a playground   **b** market   **c** car park
6. Doctors and nurses work in this place.
   a guest-house   **b** hospital   **c** factory
7. You can study lots of different subjects in this place.
   a college   **b** supermarket   **c** hotel
8. People work in this place and make things such as cars.
   a museum   **b** cafeteria   **c** factory

☑ Exam task

2 **Which notice (A–H) says this (1–5)?**
For questions (1–5), write the correct answer.

1. Everyone needs to wear a hat in this place.

2. Speak to this person if you would like to work here.

3. You can only go out this way if you work here.

4. To get to other floors, you need to walk.

5. You should not take these with you when you go out.

A
> **Swimming pool**
> Take off shoes please!
> Children don't need hats in pool

B
> **Lift not working**
> *Please use stairs*

C
> **Guests**
> Give room keys to receptionist
> before leaving the hotel

D
> Door on this floor for staff only
> **NO EXIT FOR VISITORS**

E
> Factory staff and visitors
> Keep hair covered at all times

F
> **Visitors**
> Walk this way around the top
> floor of the castle

G
> SPORTS CENTRE
> New staff needed. Phone
> manager for more information.

H
> *Please do not make calls*
> while in the hospital building

3 Complete the dialogue with your own words.
Put ONE word in each space.

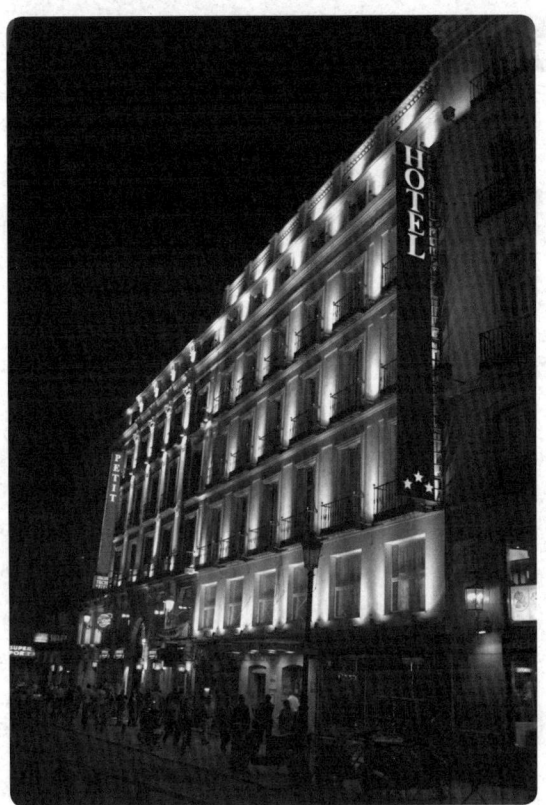

Receptionist: Good morning. Can I
(1) .... you?

Nikki: Yes please. I **(2)** .... love to go to a museum. Is there one **(3)** .... this hotel?

Receptionist: Yes. You can walk to it from here. Just go out of the hotel, **(4)** .... left, walk for about ten minutes, and you will see it on your right.

Nikki: Thank you. **(5)** .... it a big museum?

Receptionist: Yes, it's the national museum. It's very large, and there's a lot to see there.

Nikki: That's great. I want to buy some postcards.
(6) .... the museum have a shop?

Receptionist: Yes, it has a very nice shop. It **(7)** .... books, and gifts – and postcards, of course.

Nikki: Thank you very much for your help.

Receptionist: You're **(8)** .... ! Just ask me if you need anything else while you're staying here.

 Exam tips

- Quickly read the seven short texts and think about where you might see them.
- Look for words or phrases in the sentences and the short texts that have the same meaning.
- Compare each sentence with each text before you choose an answer.

Services

1 **Complete the sentences below using words from the box.**

bank	café	chemist	dentist	hotel
library	post office	tourist information		

1. I'm going to the .... to buy a stamp.

2. Is the .... open today? I need to get some cash.

3. My tooth hurts. I think I should make an appointment with my ....

4. I'm going to the .... to borrow a book about insects.

5. I've got my flight, but I still need to book a room in a .... for my holiday.

6. Is there a .... near here? I need to buy some medicine.

7. I booked a tour of the city at the .... centre.

8. Let's go to that new .... They make great hot chocolate.

2 **Read the signs. Put the number in the correct part of the table.**

Bank	Tourist information centre	Library
....	....	....

1 *Please try to return books to the correct shelf. Thank you.*

2 *Need to find a room in a hotel? We can book one for you.*

3   **Information about train and bus times at this desk only.**

4 **Need to borrow money today?** Speak to a member of staff.

5   **DVDs £1.50** *for one week.*

6 *Computer course for beginners. Starts Monday.*

7 Lost your credit card? Call this number immediately. ☎ **970097 86809**

8 **Please pay for maps in cash.**

Exam task

3

Which notice (A–H) says this (1–5)?

For questions (1–5), write the correct answer.

1. Speak to this person if you want to know how much you will pay.

2. You don't have to pay for information at this place.

3. Be careful that you have enough money for this.

4. You have to pay if you don't take these back at the right time.

5. Customers can't pay with credit cards here.

A
> **Cinema**
> We cannot change your seats after you've paid for tickets.

B
> **Library members**
> *It will cost you £1 for books you return late.*

C
> **Tourist Office**
> Free maps and guidebooks – come inside and ask.

D
> **DENTIST**
> Ask the receptionist for our price list.

E
> **Post office**
> You can pay bills here. Ask staff for more information.

F
> **Café**
> Cash only at this desk, please.

G
> **TOURISTS**
> Need dollars or euros?
> Buy them here – cash or credit cards

H
> **Petrol station**
> Make sure you can pay before filling your car!

Get it right!

Look at the sentence below. Then try to correct the mistake.

The weather is very beautiful and I stay often on the beach.

Shopping

1 Read the definitions. Then put the letters in the right order to make words.

1. This is how much you have to pay for something in a shop. (cirpe) ....
2. This is a piece of paper which you can use to pay for things. (hecequ) ....
3. This is a big shop which sells food and lots of other things. (mersteparuk) ....
4. This is what some people call a shop. (roset) ....
5. This word means something which is not cheap. (pivenexes) ....
6. This is a person who buys something in a shop. (turemocs) ....
7. If there is a problem with something you buy, you might do this with it. (gnecah) ....
8. If a shop isn't open 24 hours a day, it does this at night. (selco) ....

 Exam task

2 Read the sentences about a woman who goes shopping.
Choose the best word (A, B or C) for each space.

1. Reena would like a new pair of jeans but she doesn't want to .... too much money.
   A spend   **B** cost   **C** save

2. Reena goes into a clothes shop, and the shop .... shows her some jeans.
   A staff   **B** colleague   **C** assistant

3. Reena decides to .... on the jeans in the changing room.
   A try   **B** get   **C** turn

4. Reena likes the jeans, and is happy because they are on ....
   A discount   **B** sale   **C** market

5. Reena pays for the jeans, and asks for her ....
   A list   **B** document   **C** receipt

3a 🔊 Track 1 **Listen to the conversations. Answer the questions with a price or number from the box. You do not need all of the prices and numbers.**

10	£3	4	£12	£4.50	6	200
£11.50	£15	3	£4	2	£1.50	

1. How much does the woman need to pay? ....
2. How much does the man need to pay? ....
3. How many pens does the woman buy? ....
4. How many calendars does the man buy? ....
5. How many bottles does the woman want to buy? ....
6. How much is one kilo of cheese? ....
7. How many plates does the woman buy? ....
8. How much did the man pay for his book? ....

3b **Write a few sentences about your favourite shop or shopping centre.**

....
....
....
....
....
....
....
....
....
....
....

☑ **Exam facts**

- In this part, you read five sentences about the same topic or story.
- Each sentence has one word missing.
- You have to choose one word (A, B or C) to complete each sentence.

© Cambridge University Press and UCLES 2015

Food and drink

1a Complete the text with the correct alternatives.

Breakfast around the world

Most people agree that it is important to eat breakfast in the morning. But breakfast is different all over the world. In Japan, for example, many people have a bowl of hot **(1)** *sauce / soup* for breakfast, but in Australia most people eat cold **(2)** *cereal / dessert* with milk. Milk is used to make **(3)** *omelette / yogurt*, which lots of Americans eat in the morning. **(4)** *Curry / Coffee* is a very popular breakfast drink, and in many countries people eat toast, which is **(5)** *grilled / fried* bread, with butter. In some European countries such as Germany and Sweden, people eat cold meats such as **(6)** *ham / burger* with their bread, or sometimes cheese, but in the UK people prefer something sweet such as **(7)** *jam / juice* on their toast at breakfast time. In countries where people cook in the morning, **(8)** *cakes / eggs* are very popular, and lots of people eat them with sausages.

1b Write a few sentences about breakfast in your country.

....
....
....
....
....
....
....
....
....
....

2

Read the sentences about a student who works in a restaurant.

Choose the best word (A, B or C) for each space.

1. Franz speaks to each customer and writes their .... in his notebook.
   A order   **B** menu   **C** sign

2. Sometimes Franz needs to .... to customers what is in the dishes.
   A understand   **B** decide   **C** explain

3. The restaurant chef tries to .... the food as quickly as possible.
   A prepare   **B** improve   **C** cover

4. When the food is ready, Franz .... it to the customers.
   A leaves   **B** serves   **C** puts

5. When the customers finish eating, they ask Franz for their ....
   A price   **B** bill   **C** purse

3

Read the phrases below, and decide who is speaking. Write W (waitress) or C (customer).

1. Excuse me, could I have some more water, please? ....

2. How would you like your steak cooked, sir? ....

3. That dish comes with salad or chips. Which would you prefer? ....

4. My food is cold! Is yours okay? ....

5. I think I'm going to have a dessert. They're really good here. ....

6. Shall I take your plates now? ....

7. Could you ask the chef to make my pizza without onions, please? ....

8. Good evening. We've booked a table for six people. ....

☑ **Exam tips**

- Look at the words before and after each space.

- Try each word (A, B and C) in the space before choosing the correct answer.

- When you have completed the five sentences, read them all again to make sure they make sense.

House and home

1 Sort the words in the box into three groups. Give each group a title.

| golden | large | pale pink | purple |
| round | small | square | star |

Group 1	Group 2	Group 3 ....
....	....	....
....	....	....
....	....	....

☑ Exam task

2 **Read the sentences about Samira's new house.**
Choose the best word (A, B or C) for each space.

1. Samira's family have taken all of their .... , like sofas, to the new house.
   A luggage   **B** furniture   **C** software

2. In their old house, Samira .... a bedroom with her sister, but now she has her own bedroom.
   A included   **B** joined   **C** shared

3. Samira has put all of her things in the drawers and ....
   A cupboards   **B** shelves   **C** carpets

4. The light in Samira's room is broken, but her father says he can .... it.
   A build   **B** repair   **C** improve

5. Samira has decided to .... her new room in her favourite colour, green.
   A print   **B** fill   **C** paint

Get it right!

Look at the sentences below and choose the correct one.

Today we went to visit the Tower and last night we had a nice meal at my friend's house.

Today we went to visit the Tower and last night we had a nice meal in my friend's house.

Look at the picture of a living room. Are the sentences TRUE or FALSE?

1. There is a table between the two armchairs. ....
2. There are three black chairs around the long table. ....
3. There is a mirror between the two large windows. ....
4. One of the tables has a bowl of fruit on it. ....
5. There is a book next to the plant. ....
6. There is a lamp in the corner of the room. ....
7. The television is on the wall, near one of the windows. ....
8. There is a carpet in front of the sofa. ....

Write a few sentences about your living room.

....
....
....
....
....
....
....
....
....
....
....

Social interaction

1 Complete the questions with the correct question word(s).

1. .... is that, sitting near the door?
2. .... do you come here? Once a week?
3. .... bag is that, on the chair?
4. .... song shall we listen to first?
5. .... have you lived here?

6. .... do you think we should do?
7. .... did you buy that hat? I'd like to get one.
8. .... will we see you again?

☑ Exam facts

- This part of the test has two tasks.
- In the first task, you read what someone says, and you have to choose one reply (A, B or C) to complete the conversation.
- In the second task, you read what one person says in a longer conversation, and you have to choose the second person's replies.

© Cambridge University Press and UCLES 2015

☑ Exam task

2 Complete the five conversations.
For questions 1–5, choose A, B or C.

1. I'm sorry I didn't come to your party.
   A Yes, you are.
   B That's okay.
   C Did you?

2. Can you help me with this heavy bag, please?
   A I think it's mine.
   B No, it isn't.
   C Yes, of course.

3. I'm from Italy.
   A What's it like?
   B Is it yours?
   C Yes, you're right.

4. Thanks for the lovely present.
   A Oh, it's yours!
   B If you're sure.
   C You're welcome.

5. This is my friend Richard.
   A That was nice of him.
   B Pleased to meet you.
   C I think you should.

Now complete the conversation between two friends.

What does Sofia say to Zoe?

For questions 6–10, choose the correct letter A–H.

Zoe: Hi Sofia. Have you got any plans for the weekend?

Sofia: No, nothing special.

Zoe: Oh. Well, shall we do something together?

Sofia: **6** ....

Zoe: Why don't you come to my house to watch a film on Saturday evening?

Sofia: **7** ....

Zoe: Thanks. Shall we ask some other people too?

Sofia: **8** ....

Zoe: And I think Ada might be able to come too. I'll ask her.

Sofia: **9** ....

Zoe: Why don't you come earlier than that?

Sofia: **10** ....

Zoe: I'm sure it will be! See you on Saturday then.

A So we can chat before the film? Is an hour enough?

B That's a good idea. See you at 8 o'clock?

C Doesn't she usually work at that time?

D There's a book I need to read for college, but nothing else.

E Yeah, I'd like that. Any ideas?

F I don't think we are.

G Sure. My sister's probably free.

H OK. I'll bring some snacks and drinks.

---

3 ▶ Pieter asks his friend Sami to come to his house for dinner. Tick (✓) the two polite responses to the question.

Pieter: Would you like to come to my house for dinner on Sunday, Sami?

Sami:
1. No, I can't. ☐
2. Thanks, that's a lovely idea. ☐
3. I'm afraid I'm busy then. ☐
4. No, I would not like to. ☐

Feelings, opinions and experiences

1 Put the words into the correct order to make sentences and questions.

1. Japan / been / to / never / have / I / .

   ....

2. here / she / worked / years / for / has / three / .

   ....

3. mountain / have / a / climbed / ever / you / ?

   ....

4. just / mum / have / I / seen / your/ .

   ....

5. the / started / film / yet / has / ?

   ....

6. dinner / already / I / finished / have / my / .

   ....

7. for / we / lived / months / have / here / two / .

   ....

8. to / wanted / I / him / always / meet / have / !

   ....

☑ *Exam task*

2 Complete the five conversations.

For questions 1–5, choose A, B or C.

1. I met my new neighbour today!

   A What's she like?

   B Does she know?

   C Has she been there?

2. Did you have a good evening?

   A No, I don't think it was.

   B Yes, lovely, thank you.

   C Thanks, but I'm busy.

3. Where do you prefer to sit?

   A Is it on this side?

   B Yes, I think we should.

   C Near the window, please.

4. Have you ever been to the ballet?

   A There aren't any tickets.

   B It's a great idea!

   C Not until today!

5. I've never seen that boy before.

   A Shall I ask him?

   B I think he's new.

   C It isn't his.

Now complete the conversation between two friends.
What does Kim say to Serena?
For questions 6–10, choose the correct letter A–H.

Serena: Hi Kim! I haven't seen you for ages!

Kim: Yes, I know. It's been so long.

Serena: Have you been ill?

Kim: **6** ....

Serena: Oh, lucky you! Where did you go?

Kim: **7** ....

Serena: I didn't know that. Was it your first visit?

Kim: **8** ....

Serena: No, but I'd like to. When is the best time to go?

Kim: **9** ....

Serena: That's good to know. So, did you take any photos?

Kim: **10** ....

Serena: Yeah, I'd love that. Thanks.

A I did – in Thailand!

B Of course! I'll show them to you when you have some time.

C Probably when it's winter here.

D I was at home at the weekend.

E Yes, that's true. Not since last month.

F To Australia. My brother lives there.

G No! I was on holiday!

H Actually, I've been there before. Have you ever been?

---

3 🔊 Track 2 **Listen to the conversations. Answer the questions.**

1. When will they go shopping? ....
2. Do the speakers agree with each other? ....
3. Does the man like his new phone? ....
4. What time will they leave? ....
5. Did the woman like the film? ....
6. What do they decide to eat? ....
7. What will the man wear? ....
8. Does the man prefer his laptop or the woman's laptop? ....

☑ **Exam tips**

- In the first task, read the first part of each conversation and think what the second person might say.
- Then look at options, A, B and C, and decide which one completes the conversation.
- In the second task, when choosing the correct option, look at the sentences before and after the gap.
- When you complete the conversations, read them again to make sure they make sense.

Hobbies and leisure

1 Complete these sentences with the correct word. The first letter of the word is given to help you.

1. A cinema is a place where people go to watch f ....
2. If you want to see a p .... you can go to a theatre.
3. My hobby is photography. I've just bought a new c................ .
4. My younger brother loves c................ and he wants to be a chef when he's older.
5. I'm going out for a m........... tonight, to my favourite restaurant.
6. I'm interested in art. I often go to a m .... to look at paintings.
7. My friend spends a lot of time on his computer playing v .... games.
8. I play the piano. Do you play a musical i .... ?

☑ Exam task

2 Complete the five conversations.
For questions 1–5, choose A, B or C.

1. What did you think of that book?

   A I forgot to bring it.
   B It isn't mine.
   C I enjoyed it.

2. Shall we have a picnic?

   A I'd prefer a barbecue.
   B Yes, I think it might.
   C I'm going to a party.

3. Would you like a cup of tea?

   A Yes, I'd love to, thanks.
   B Coffee for me, please.
   C I like it a lot.

4. I prefer this car to your old one.

   A Have you?
   B That's it!
   C Me too!

5. Suzy doesn't like her new job.

   A That's a shame.
   B No, it isn't.
   C Oh, I do!

Now complete the conversation between two friends.

What does Malik say to Daniel?

For questions 6–10, choose the correct letter A–H.

Daniel:	What do you like doing in your free time, Malik?
Malik:	Well, I really like music.
Daniel:	Yeah, me too. Do you ever go to concerts?
Malik:	**6** ....
Daniel:	Well, I'm going to one this Saturday. And it's free!
Malik:	**7** ....
Daniel:	Do you know the park near my house?
Malik:	**8** ....
Daniel:	That's it. There's going to be music, and food too. But you have to pay for the food!
Malik:	**9** ....
Daniel:	No, it's in the afternoon. It starts at 3 o'clock. Why don't you come with me and my friends?
Malik:	**10** ....
Daniel:	Yeah, that's fine. See you there.

A I think so. Is it behind the cinema?

B Of course! Is it in the evening?

C Maybe watch films. But I don't have much free time.

D I've never been there before.

E I read sometimes. And I play the guitar. I love music!

F Thanks. I'd like that. Shall I text you when I get to the park?

G They're usually too expensive for me.

H That sounds great. Where is it?

---

3 **Complete the sentences with the correct alternatives.**

1. I don't *mind / care* classical music, but I prefer pop.
2. I *nearly / quite* like art, especially modern art.
3. I enjoy playing music *most / more* than listening to it.
4. Jack *really / very* loves films, and goes to the cinema a lot.
5. Stan doesn't watch TV *many / much*. He prefers going out.
6. What's your *best / favourite* type of food?
7. Al doesn't *like / love* that new restaurant near his house at all.
8. I like camping – *also / even* when it rains.

◎ Get it right!

Look at the sentence below. Then try to correct the mistake.

There are lots of things to see here, and I already saw the Statue of Liberty and the American Museum of Natural History.

The natural world

1 Match the words in the box to the correct definition.

desert	field	forest	island	lake	mountains	plants	river

1. a large area of water, often in a park ....

2. a very large area which has lots of trees in it ....

3. a piece of land with water all around it ....

4. trees and flowers are examples of these ....

5. a very dry area where it doesn't rain much ....

6. a long area of water that often ends in the sea ....

7. a farmer grows things or puts his animals here ....

8. these are very tall and often have snow at the top ....

☑ Exam facts

- In this part, you read a text – for example, a short newspaper or magazine article.
- You have to answer seven questions.
- These may be Right, Wrong, Doesn't say or A, B or C questions.

☑ Exam task

2 Read the article about three people who are interested in nature.
Answer the questions. For questions 1–7, choose A, B or C.

My love of nature

A Sarah

When I was a child at school, I collected books about nature. My classmates and friends all spent their free time playing computer games, so to them I was a bit strange. I loved learning about animals from other countries, but as I got older I found out that my own country has interesting nature too, and that's what I like studying now. I do lots of drawings of nature, and I put them on my blog.

B Pilar

I love birds and animals because of all the visits to forests and lakes we made when I was at school. It's a shame that things have changed now. Children these days don't learn enough about nature, so lots of them are afraid of insects, for example. I have a great job because of my love of nature. I'm a nature photographer. It's brilliant, except for the early mornings!

C Lia

A few years ago I read a blog with beautiful photos of animals, birds and plants, which made me start really looking at what lives around us. It was just a hobby at first, but now it's my job as I visit schools and give talks about nature. I love it. The only problem is if I am asked to draw a picture. I enjoy it, but I'm terrible at drawing! I'm going to take some lessons to try to get better.

1. Who became interested in nature from seeing someone else's blog?

   A Sarah   **B** Pilar   **C** Lia

2. Who says there is something about her job that she doesn't like?

   A Sarah   **B** Pilar   **C** Lia

3. Whose friends thought that her hobby was unusual?

   A Sarah   **B** Pilar   **C** Lia

4. Who became interested in nature because of school trips?

   A Sarah   **B** Pilar   **C** Lia

5. Who says that the type of nature she is interested in has changed?

   A Sarah   **B** Pilar   **C** Lia

6. Who wants to improve her pictures of nature?

   A Sarah   **B** Pilar   **C** Lia

7. Who thinks that young people should learn more about nature at school?

   A Sarah   **B** Pilar   **C** Lia

3 ▶ **Complete the conversation with phrases from the boxes.**

Adam: Do you live in a town, Ben?

Ben: No, in the countryside. And I love it.

Adam: **(1)** .... I lived in the countryside when I was a child, but I prefer towns.

Ben: Oh! Why is that?

Adam: Well, in the countryside you're so far away from schools, shops and friends' houses.

Ben: **(2)** .... You get more exercise because you have to walk more!

Adam: **(3)** .... You spend a lot of time in your car, driving everywhere!

Ben: But the traffic is much worse in towns. Towns are too noisy and busy.

Adam: **(4)** .... The countryside is boring!

Ben: **(5)** .... You can go walking, cycling, fishing – there are lots of things to do!

Adam: Yes – I can do them during short visits to the countryside! But I prefer to live in a town.

Ben: **(6)** .... I'm sure the view from my window is better that yours.

Adam: You're probably right. It's true that the countryside is beautiful, but I enjoy being with lots of people.

Ben: And that's what I hate!

Adam: Everyone is different, I suppose.

Ben: We certainly are!

Ben	**Adam**
a No, it isn't.	d No, you don't.
b Yes, but that's a good thing.	e Really? I don't understand that.
c Well, I don't.	f That's what I like!

Education and study

1 Complete the text below with the school subjects. Use the letters in brackets to help you.

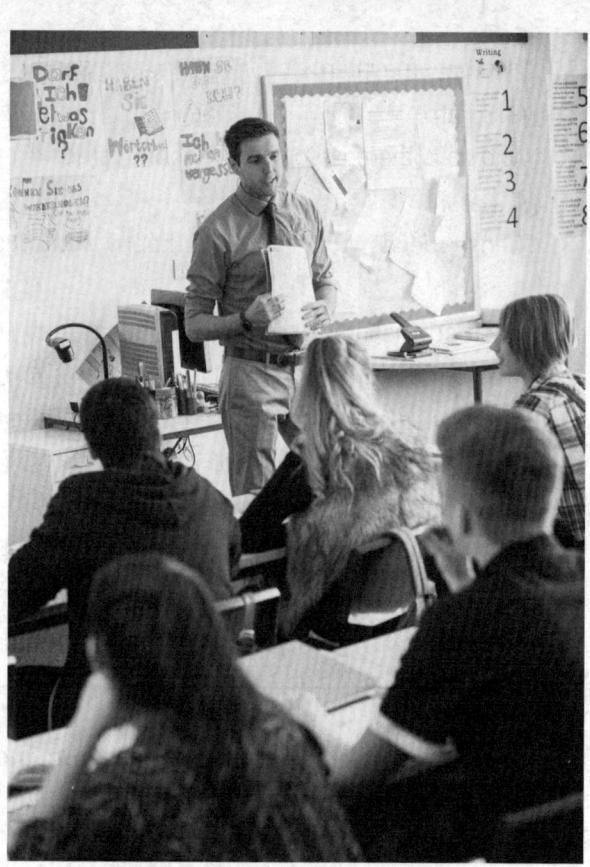

There are lots of different subjects you can study at university. If you are good at **(1)** .... (gauselnag), you may decide to study French, Arabic or Chinese. If you like learning about how things work, then you probably find science subjects such as **(2)** .... (gibyolo), **(3)** .... (myshecrit) or **(4)** .... (shycips) interesting. People who are interested in things which happened a long time ago should study **(5)** .... (osriyth), but if you prefer learning about rivers, mountains and the different countries of the world, then you should choose **(6)** .... (regopaygh). People who are good with numbers often decide to study **(7)** .... (shacamittem), and those who want to become doctors take a course in **(8)** .... (necmidei).

☑ Exam task

2 Read the article about a new type of school desk.

Answer the questions. For questions 1–7, choose A, B or C.

We know that sitting down all the time is bad for us, and for this reason, standing desks have become quite popular in offices. A 'standing desk' is higher than a normal desk, so that people can do their work standing up. Now, schools are starting to use them too. Over the last few years, students in schools all over the world have tried these desks. But students don't have to stand for the whole school day, because standing desks come with stools – high chairs without backs – so they can sit down when they want to.

Teachers at a school in the US which tried the standing desks say that students listened to the teacher more during lessons when they used the desks. The teachers were surprised to see that younger students used the stools less than the older students. They think that this is because older students have already spent years sitting at desks, so it is difficult for them to change what they do.

So will all schools start using standing desks soon? Well, they aren't cheap, so most schools will probably use their old desks for quite a few more years first.

1. Standing desks are taller than normal desks.

   A Right   **B** Wrong   **C** Doesn't say

2. More offices than schools use standing desks.

   A Right   **B** Wrong   **C** Doesn't say

3. Standing desks have been tried in only one country.

   A Right   **B** Wrong   **C** Doesn't say

4. If a class use standing desks, the teacher tells the students when to sit down.

   A Right   **B** Wrong   **C** Doesn't say

5. Students who use standing desks work better in groups.

   A Right   **B** Wrong   **C** Doesn't say

6. Older students like sitting down at desks more than younger students.

   A Right   **B** Wrong   **C** Doesn't say

7. Standing desks are less expensive than normal desks.

   A Right   **B** Wrong   **C** Doesn't say

3   **Complete the sentences with the correct alternatives.**

1. I *broken / break / broke* my pen yesterday.
2. When I was little I didn't *known / know / knew* how to write.
3. I *ridden / rode / ride* my new bike to college yesterday.
4. I was so tired when I got home from school that I *lain / lie / lay* down and fell asleep.
5. I *took / taken / take* my exams last week.
6. We *given / give / gave* our teacher a present at the end of the year.
7. Did you *saw / see / seen* your friend at college?
8. I didn't *go / went / gone* to school until I was seven years old.

☑ *Exam tips*

- Quickly read the text before you answer the questions.
- The questions are in the same order as the information in the text.
- Compare the questions and options to the text carefully.
- Don't think an answer is right just because you see the same word in the text and the question.

Travel and holidays

1 Compete the advice about plane travel. The first letter of each word is given to help you.

If you are going to travel to a different country, you need to have a **(1)** p .... When you are packing, try not to put too much in your **(2)** l .... Try to get to the **(3)** a .... a few hours before your flight so that you won't **(4)** m .... it, and so that you get a good **(5)** s .... on the plane. Take something to read, as there may be a **(6)** d .... if the flight is late, or if the weather is bad. During the flight, be polite to other **(7)** p .... , and remember to listen to the instructions which the **(8)** p .... and other airline staff give you.

☑ Exam tasks

2 Read the article about three people's holidays.

Answer the questions. For questions 1–7, choose A, B or C.

My last holiday

A Max

I went on holiday with my friends. The flight was fine, but it took two hours by bus to reach the hotel – I didn't enjoy that! The hotel was noisy and the staff weren't friendly, but it didn't matter because we spent all our time on the beach, a short walk away. We tried lots of new dishes in the restaurants in the town. It was hard to sleep with such high temperatures, but we had a fantastic time, and the best thing was, we spent almost nothing once we arrived!

B Felipe

The drive to our hotel from the airport was along lovely country roads. The hotel my wife and I stayed in was quite expensive. The people who worked there were wonderful, but I wasn't so sure about the hotel restaurant – the desserts were fine, but the main courses weren't very good. It was cloudy and rainy most days, but we went to walk in the countryside, not to lie on a beach.

C Nikhil

My family and I drove across the USA last year. We stayed in lots of different hotels. I don't know how much we spent because my parents paid. There was a lot of driving, but my dad enjoyed that. The weather was fantastic, and I couldn't believe the differences in what people ate from place to place. It was good to be with the family, because there was always someone to talk to, or to do things with.

1. Who was surprised about the variety of food on holiday?

    A Max   **B** Felipe   **C** Nikhil

2. Who thought that part of their journey was too long?

    A Max   **B** Felipe   **C** Nikhil

3. Who liked travelling with a group of people?

    A Max   **B** Felipe   **C** Nikhil

4. Who was happy with the cost of their holiday?

    A Max   **B** Felipe   **C** Nikhil

5. Who thought the hotel staff were good?

    A Max   **B** Felipe   **C** Nikhil

6. Who was unhappy with some of the food they ate?

    A Max   **B** Felipe   **C** Nikhil

7. Who says that the weather was a problem at times?

    A Max   **B** Felipe   **C** Nikhil

---

3 ◀)) Track 3 **Listen to the conversations. Are the sentences TRUE or FALSE?**

1. The woman needs to drive north to get to the airport. ....

2. The man needs to go straight on at the roundabout. ....

3. The restaurant is a long way from the hotel. ....

4. The man knows a faster way to get to the beach. ....

5. The man and the woman need to go south. ....

6. The man and the woman need to turn left to get to the market. ....

7. The hotel is on the road where the man already is. ....

8. The woman needs to turn right immediately. ....

◉ Get it right!

Look at the sentence below. Then try to correct the mistake.

I've seen my brother yesterday.

Sports and games

1a Put the sports and games into the correct part of the table.

> chess   exercise   fishing
> football   golf   karate   skiing
>   swimming   tennis

go	play	do
....	....	....
....	....	....
....		

1b Look at the table. Are there any rules about which verb to use with which nouns? Can you add more sports or games to the table?

☑️ Exam tasks

2 Read the article about tennis.

Choose the best word (A, B or C) for each space.

Tennis

The English name 'tennis' comes from the French word 'tenez', **(1)** .... means 'to hold'. When the first games of tennis **(2)** .... played hundreds of years ago, people used **(3)** .... hands to hit the ball. Now, of course, we use rackets.

A player **(4)** .... to get four points to win a game, and six games to win a set. In women's tennis, a player wins the match **(5)** .... winning two sets. This is often the same in men's tennis, **(6)** .... in some competitions men need to win three sets to win a match.

If two people play tennis against each **(7)** .... , it is called a singles match. If **(8)** .... are two players on each side, it is called a doubles match.

1	**A** who	**B** that	**C** which
2	**A** is	**B** were	**C** was
3	**A** their	**B** his	**C** your
4	**A** can	**B** must	**C** has
5	**A** by	**B** at	**C** for
6	**A** so	**B** but	**C** with
7	**A** one	**B** other	**C** own
8	**A** there	**B** here	**C** where

3a Complete the sentences with the correct alternatives.

1. When I *cycled / was cycling* in the park, I *saw / was seeing* Cristina.
2. I hurt my leg while I *played / was playing* football.
3. I *called / was calling* you at 8 o'clock last night, but you didn't answer. What *did you do / were you doing*?
4. We were so late for the match that they *already played / were already playing* when we arrived.
5. We *played / were playing* tennis when it started raining, so we *stopped / were stopping*.
6. *Did you go / Were you going* skiing when you were in Austria?
7. I *forgot / was forgetting* to bring my badminton racket, but Fay had two so she *lent / was lending* me one.
8. I *met / was meeting* a really interesting man when I *fished / was fishing* yesterday.

3b Write a few sentences about a sport that you like.

....
....
....
....
....
....
....
....
....
....

> ☑ **Exam facts**
>
> - In this part, you read a short text – for example a newspaper or magazine article.
> - There are eight missing words in the text.
> - You have to choose the correct word (A, B or C) to complete each space.
>
> © Cambridge University Press and UCLES 2015

Entertainment and media

1 ❯ **Match the musical words with the definitions.**

1.	To play this instrument you have to hit it.	**a** practice
2.	A group of people who play music together.	**b** opera
3.	A person who plays an instrument.	**c** drum
4.	Lots of songs together by the same band or artist.	**d** band
5.	You need to do this a lot when you learn to play an instrument.	**e** album
6.	You touch the black and white parts of this instrument to play it.	**f** record
7.	A musical play where people sing the words.	**g** musician
8.	People do this with their music so that other people can listen to it.	**h** keyboard

 Exam task

2 ❯ **Read the article about a rock concert.**

Choose the best word (A, B or C) for each space.

A rock concert

Famous groups don't come to my town very often,
(1) .... when my brother showed me a poster for a concert by my favourite band, I was really excited. We asked some friends **(2)** .... they wanted to come with **(3)** .... , and then we bought the tickets.

A few weeks later, we met at my house and got a bus to the concert, **(4)** .... was in a stadium. We didn't know the first band who played – they weren't famous. Their music was okay, **(5)** .... not great. I just **(6)** .... wait for my favourite group to play. When they finally came onto the stage everyone started **(7)** .... They played all of their best songs, and of course the crowd all sang too. I don't think I will **(8)** .... forget that night.

1	**A** because		**B** so		**C** except	
2	**A** if		**B** that		**C** as	
3	**A** us		**B** them		**C** we	
4	**A** what		**B** who		**C** which	
5	**A** or		**B** but		**C** and	
6	**A** shouldn't		**B** mustn't		**C** couldn't	
7	**A** shout		**B** shouting		**C** shouted	
8	**A** ever		**B** always		**C** never	

Read the suggestions. Choose the TWO correct answers from a, b or c.

1. Why don't we go to a museum at the weekend?

   a I don't want to do that at all.

   b I'd prefer to go to a concert.

   c Okay, that sounds good.

2. Shall we have dinner together on Friday?

   a I'm busy then, but maybe another day?

   b I'm sorry, I'm busy then.

   c I don't think we will, no.

3. Let's watch a film.

   a No, let's not.

   b No, let's do something else.

   c No, not just at the moment.

4. How about going to a concert on Sunday?

   a Yes, I'd love to.

   b Yes, that's right.

   c Yes, that's a great idea.

5. Why don't you ask Maya to come to the opera?

   a I don't think she likes opera.

   b Because I don't like opera.

   c I might do that!

6. Shall we listen to some music?

   a Maybe later?

   b Yeah, lovely!

   c We shall not.

7. I'll take a photo, shall I?

   a No, don't worry.

   b No, you won't.

   c No, I'll do it.

8. Let's go dancing at the weekend.

   a Sure. Why not?

   b Why should we?

   c That's not a bad idea!

☑ **Exam tips**

- Quickly read the text before you choose your answers.
- Try each word (A, B and C) in the space before you choose the correct answer.
- Read the whole sentence carefully when you choose an answer.

Transport

1a Complete the table with the comparative and superlative forms of the adjectives.

adjective	comparative	superlative
big	....	....
bad	....	....
fast	....	....
dirty	....	....
modern	....	....
healthy	....	....
popular	....	....
crowded	....	....

1b Complete each sentence with a word from Exercise 1a.

1. The traffic is .... during the week than at weekends, because everyone is going to work.
2. Wow! I thought my car needed a wash, but yours is even .... than mine!
3. The trains in this city are the .... I've even been on. There are so many people on them!
4. I get home later in the evening now that I walk, but it's .... for me than driving.
5. There's a lot of space in this car – it's .... than the one you had before.
6. In cities which have a river, boats are quite a .... way to get around.
7. A hundred years ago, the .... car in the world could only travel at 136 km/h.
8. We have a lovely .... railway station now – much better than the old one.

☑ Exam task

2 Read the article about travelling by car.

Choose the best word (A, B or C) for each space.

Better ways to travel

Millions of us use our cars every day to get to work, college or school. Travelling by car is fast and comfortable, but not good for the world **(1)** .... us. So what **(2)** .... we do? One possibility is to share car journeys. If you have neighbours **(3)** .... travel to the same place, **(4)** .... together in one car. Two or three people travelling together is **(5)** .... than two or three cars making the same journey with only one person in **(6)** .... car.

Of course, cars are not the **(7)** .... way to travel. It's usually possible to make your journey by bus, tram or train, especially in a town or city. And if your journey is short, what **(8)** .... walking or going by bike? You'll get fit, and save money too!

1	**A** beside		**B** across		**C** around
2	**A** can		**B** would		**C** may
3	**A** what		**B** which		**C** who
4	**A** go		**B** gone		**C** going
5	**A** good		**B** better		**C** best
6	**A** other		**B** each		**C** any
7	**A** only		**B** single		**C** alone
8	**A** with		**B** to		**C** about

3a Read the predictions about the future. Look at the <u>underlined</u> phrases and number them 1–5
(1 = most likely to happen, 5 = least likely to happen).

a <u>I think</u> plane journeys will be shorter in the future. ....

b <u>It's possible</u> that / <u>Maybe</u> we'll all have flying cars in the future. ....

c <u>I'm very sure</u> / <u>I'm certain</u> that our journeys to work will be shorter, because trains are getting
faster. ....

d <u>I'm not sure</u> if we'll still travel by train a hundred years from now. ....

e <u>I'm sure</u> we won't use petrol in our cars for much longer. ....

3b Write five sentences about what you think will happen to transport in the future. Use the
phrases from Exercise 3a.

1. ....

2. ....

3. ....

4. ....

5. ....

Get it right!

Look at the sentences below and choose the correct one.

The most thing I like about it is the camera.

The thing I like most about it is the camera.

The weather

1

Put the letters of the English alphabet in the correct part of the table according to how they are pronounced.

/eɪ/	/iː/	/e/	/aɪ/	/oʊ/	/uː/	/ɑː/
a	b	f	i	o	q	r
h	c	l	_		_	
_	d	m			_	
_	e	n				
	_	_				
	_	_				
	_					
	_					

☑ Exam task

2

Read the descriptions of some words about the weather.

What is the word for each one?

The first letter is already there. There is one space for each other letter in the word.

1. These are white, grey or black, and you can see them in the sky.   c _ _ _ _ _
2. When the weather is very cold, water changes to this.   i _ _
3. In this type of weather it is difficult to see where you are going.   f _ _ _ _
4. This is what the weather is like in the desert, because it doesn't rain much.   d _ _
5. During one of these it rains a lot and it is very windy.   s _ _ _ _

3a Match the comments about the weather to the replies.

1. It's going to be hot today.	**a** Me too. It's fun to play in.
2. The weather was great at the weekend.	**b** Really? Oh, I'll change my clothes then.
3. Do you think it'll rain later?	**c** No. I was asleep.
4. What's the weather like where you live?	**d** But it's so different today!
5. I love the snow!	**e** Yes, take your umbrella.
6. Did you hear the thunderstorm last night?	**f** It's warm and sunny here, as usual.

3b Write a few sentences about the weather in your country.

....

....

....

....

....

....

....

....

....

....

 Exam facts

- In this part, you read the descriptions of five words.

- You have to write the five words and spell them correctly.

- You can see the first letter of each word and the number of missing letters.

Clothes

1 Complete the table with the words from the box.

| boots | cap | hat | shoes |
| shorts | tights | trainers | trousers |

feet	head	legs
....	....	....
....	....	....
....		....

☑ **Exam task**

2 Read the descriptions of some words about clothes.

What is the word for each one?

The first letter is already there. There is one space for each other letter in the word.

1. This is often made of wool, and keeps you warm in cold weather.   s _ _ _ _ _ _
2. Your wear these on your hands.   g _ _ _ _ _
3. This covers your legs and is usually worn by women.   s _ _ _ _
4. This stops your trousers falling down.   b _ _ _
5. You wear this around your neck in cold weather.   s _ _ _ _

3a Complete the sentences with the correct alternatives.

1. Remy, is this scarf *you / your / yours* ?
2. *What / Who / Which* does this jumper belong to?
3. My cousin is only two, but she can already dress *herself / itself / yourself*.
4. I've brought a spare swimming costume, because I thought *someone / anyone / no one* might forget theirs.
5. I can't find my belt. Do you have *this / one / it* I can borrow?
6. I need to buy some ties for work. I don't have *many / much / more*.

3b Write a few sentences about what you are wearing today.

....
....
....
....
....
....
....
....
....
....

☑ **Exam tips**

- All the words are about the same topic. The instructions of the task tell you what the topic is.
- The answers are normally nouns. They are often singular, but some can be plural.
- Only write one letter in each space, and don't leave any spaces empty.

People

1 Read the definitions. Are the sentences TRUE or FALSE?

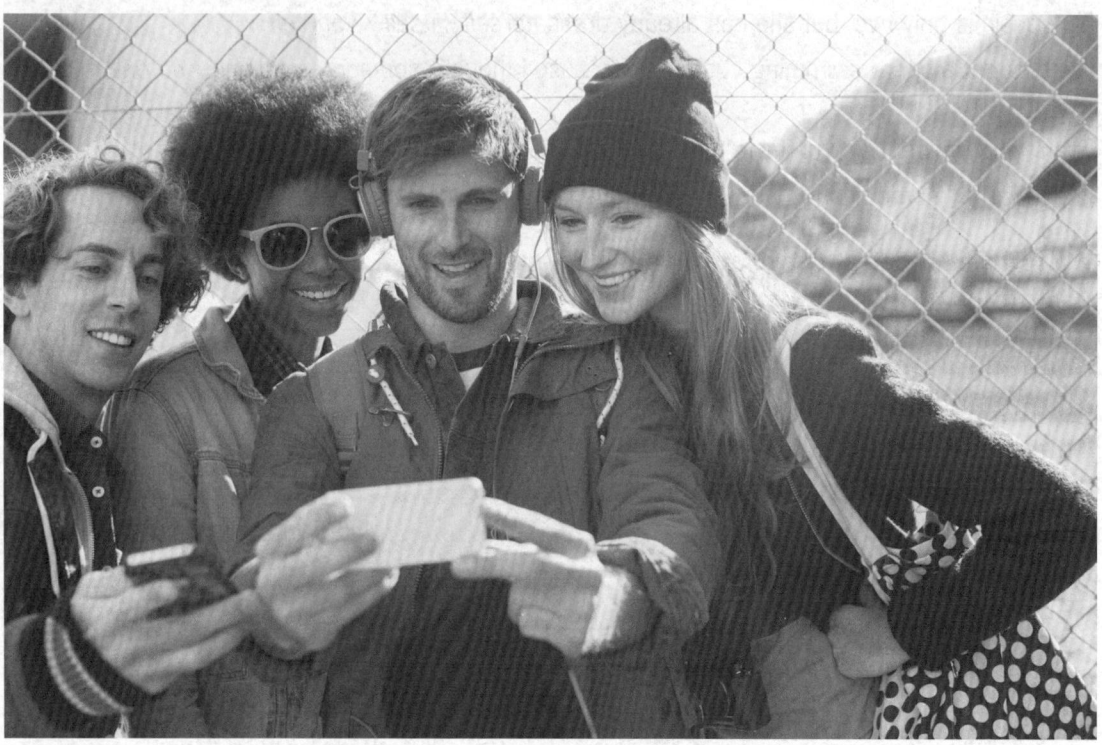

1. A beard is the hair on a man's face, under his mouth. ....

2. Someone who is fair has dark hair or skin. ....

3. Terrible means really good. ....

4. Horrible is used to describe something or someone which is not nice at all. ....

5. If someone is fun, other people like spending time with them. ....

☑ Exam task

2 Read the descriptions of some words used to describe people.

What is the word for each one?

The first letter is already there. There is one space for each other letter in the word.

1. This word is used for someone who isn't very tall.   s _ _ _ _

2. This means attractive or nice to look at.   p _ _ _ _ _

3. A person who can pick up heavy things is this.   s _ _ _ _ _

4. This word is the opposite of old.   y _ _ _ _

5. This means quite thin.   s _ _ _

3a Read the sentences about people. Write *N* (negative) or *P* (positive).

1. My sister is so lazy! .....
2. The person I spoke to on the phone was polite. .....
3. My new neighbour is very pleasant. .....
4. I met a very boring man at that party last night. .....
5. What a sweet little boy! .....
6. Your friend is really funny! .....

3b Write a few sentences about someone in your family or a friend.

....
....
....
....
....
....
....
....
....

 Get it right!

Look at the sentence below. Then try to correct the mistake.

Thank you for inviting for a meal.

Daily life

1 Complete the gaps in the text with the correct form of the verbs in the box.

am / is	close / closes	have / has
need / needs	take / takes	walk / walks
want / wants	work / works	

Every day I wake up at 8 am, and **(1)** .... a bus into town. I eat breakfast at a café, and then **(2)** .... to my family's shop. I **(3)** .... in the shop, helping my father. He **(4)** .... the manager of the shop. We **(5)** .... lunch at about 12:30 pm and Dad **(6)** .... the shop at 5 pm. I like my job, and I know Dad **(7)** .... me, but in the future I **(8)** .... to travel, so I'm saving money to pay for that.

☑ Exam task

2 Complete the emails. Write ONE word for each space.

● ● ●   **Reply**   **Forward**

Hi Jenni,
How are you? Is your new life **(1)** .... Canada going well? **(2)** .... is your university course like? **(3)** .... you made new friends? **(4)** .... you think you might come back for a visit soon? **(5)** .... you have time, write to me.
Clara

● ● ●   **Reply**   **Forward**

Hi Clara!
I'm fine, thanks. I've **(6)** .... here for a month now. It was quite difficult for the first few weeks **(7)** .... I didn't know anyone, but now that I know more people, I'm starting **(8)** .... enjoy myself. I'm sure I **(9)** .... come home for a few weeks at the end of **(10)** .... year. I really want to see my friends and family!
Keep writing to me!
Jenni

3a Complete Jenni's next email to Clara with the correct alternatives.

●●●   Reply   Forward

Dear Clara,
You asked me (1) *that / what* I do every day. Well, I get up early (2) *because / so* my
first class is (3) *at / in* 8 am. I drive to the university. (4) *After / When* I'm not in class,
I usually go to the library to study and I meet friends (5) *with / for* lunch. In the evenings
(6) *there / here* are concerts and sometimes parties. I go to some of (7) *they / them* with
my friends, (8) *but / as* I also study a lot.

3b Imagine that a friend has asked you what you do each day. Write an email to them about your typical day.

....
....
....
....
....
....
....
....
....
....

☑ **Exam facts**

- In this part, you read two short texts. These are usually two messages.
- There are ten missing words in the texts.
- You have to write the ten missing words.

© Cambridge University Press and UCLES 2015

Social interaction

1 **Complete the sentences with the correct alternatives.**

1. I *would / may* see him later, but I'm not sure.
2. *May / Can* you swim a kilometre?
3. Do you think I *should / shall* invite him?
4. I *would / might* go to the party if I'm not too tired.
5. *Could / Would* you like to come to dinner tomorrow?
6. My brother *shouldn't / couldn't* walk until he was nearly two!
7. *Shall / Would* I help you get lunch ready?
8. Excuse me – you *mustn't / might not* smoke in here!

2a **Complete the conversation with the correct form of the verb in brackets.**

Gleb: Hi, Jan. I **(1)** .... (not / see) you for ages! What **(2)** .... (you / do) here?

Jan: I **(3)** .... (visit) my sister. She **(4)** .... (live) here for about three months.

Gleb: Oh, great! And **(5)** .... (you / still / study) at college?

Jan: Yes, but not Maths. I **(6)** .... (do) business now. What about you?

Gleb: I **(7)** .... (work) in an office at the moment, but I **(8)** .... (want) to go travelling next year.

Jan: Well, good luck with that. It was nice to see you, Gleb!

2b **Write a few sentences about your plans for the weekend.**

....
....
....
....
....
....
....
....
....
....

3

Complete the emails. Write ONE word for each space.

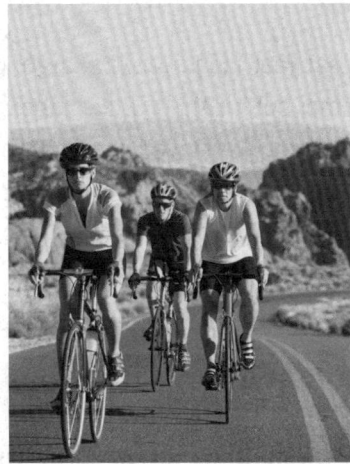

● ● ●   <u>Reply</u>   <u>Forward</u>

Hi Kris
I'm going cycling with my brother on Sunday. Would you
(1) .... to come? Don't worry if you don't (2) ....
a good bike – we've got (3) .... you can borrow. We'll
take a picnic (4) .... we won't need to eat in a café.
Let (5) .... know if you want to come.
Ali

● ● ●   <u>Reply</u>   <u>Forward</u>

Hi Ali
That's a great idea. Thanks (6) .... offering me a bike, but I got a new one a few
weeks (7) .... I'll bring lunch and something to drink. (8) .... there anything
else that I should bring? Also, (9) .... you know what time we'll be home? I need to
know (10) .... I'm going out in the evening.
Kris

✓ **Exam tips**

- Quickly read the texts before you write the missing words.
- Look at the words that come before and after the space and think about what kind of word you need to write – for example a noun, verb, preposition, etc.
- Only write one word in each space.
- When you finish, read the texts again to make sure they make sense.

Travel and holidays

1 Complete the text with the correct form of the verbs in brackets.

Last year I **(1)** .... (go) on holiday to France. We **(2)** .... (drive) there, which took a long time, but it **(3)** .... (be) good because we **(4)** .... (see) a lot of beautiful countryside on the way. We stayed in a lovely house which **(5)** .... (have) a really big swimming pool. Every day we **(6)** .... (get) up late and **(7)** .... (spend) all day in the sun. We **(8)** .... (eat) fantastic food too. I would like to go to the same place again next year.

☑ Exam task

2 Complete the email. Write ONE word for each space.

Reply   Forward

Hi Mum and Dad,
I hope everyone is OK at home. I arrived in New Zealand yesterday. On the plane I sat next
(1) .... a really nice woman **(2)** .... told me about lots of places I **(3)** ....
visit while I'm here. And I found a place to stay **(4)** .... isn't too expensive.
I'm going to be in New Zealand **(5)** .... a month, and then I'm going to fly to
(6) .... USA. Dad, **(7)** .... you remember to tell **(8)** .... friend Patricia
in San Francisco that I will be there next month? Has she said **(9)** .... it's okay for
me to stay **(10)** .... her?
I'll write again soon.
Sonia

© Cambridge University Press 2017

3

Put the words in the correct order to make questions and sentences about holiday plans.

1. year / you / are / this / where / holiday / on / going / ?

....

2. to / the / we / be / at / by / airport / ten / need / .

....

3. year / like / to / next / to / Germany / would / I / go / .

....

4. airport / are / how / the / you / to / getting / ?

....

5. to / family / I / China / going / with / am / my / .

....

6. you / long / will / how / there / stay / ?

....

7. small / a / we / hotel / to / are / stay / in / going / .

....

8. by / you / yourself / going / are / travelling / ?

....

 Get it right!

Look at the sentence below. Then try to correct the mistake.

Now I write a postcard to you and then I'm going to lunch at the new restaurant on the beach.

Hobbies and leisure

1 Match the sentences with the type of information they give.

1. I'll wait for you outside the cinema.
2. It starts at two thirty, so be there by two.
3. Ari's coming, so there'll be three of us.
4. With our student discount, it's six pounds.
5. We're going to see *Gate to the Forest*.
6. Let's go by bus.
7. It's on March 14th.
8. We're eating at Dan's Pizza Place.

a how to get somewhere
b number of people
c time to meet
d name of the film
e name of the restaurant
f place to meet
g price to pay
h date of event

☑ Exam task

2 Read the advertisement and the email.

Fill in the information in Jaya's notes.

Highstep Dance School

Jazz, ballet and street dance

Class dates: September 3rd to October 29th.
Classes for beginners and advanced students.
Small classes – no more than five in a group.

£5 per class or £30 for the term

● ● ●   **Reply**   **Forward**
From: Hannah   **To: Jaya**

About our ballet dance lessons – the advanced class at Star Dance School is full! There's another school called *Highstep*. Can you call them and book for the two of us? Let's pay for the whole term – it's cheaper!

Jaya's Notes
Dance Classes

Type of dance: *ballet*
Name of school: **1** ....
Our level: **2** ....
Number of people to book for: **3** ....
Date of first class: **4** ....
Price I'll pay: **5** ....

3a 🔊 **Track 4** **Listen to the conversations. Are the sentences TRUE or FALSE?**

1. The woman likes going to the beach. ....
2. The man likes his new hobby. ....
3. Dancing is the man's favourite activity. ....
4. The woman would like to go on holiday. ....
5. The woman wants to go camping. ....
6. The man likes parties. ....
7. The man wants to have a barbecue. ....
8. The woman would like the man to take a photo of her. ....

3b **Write a few sentences about hobbies you would like to try.**

....
....
....
....
....
....
....
....
....
....

☑ **Exam facts**

- In this part, you read two short texts.
- You have to find five pieces of information (words and numbers) in the texts.
- You use this information to complete some notes.

Sport and activities

 1

Complete the sentences with the correct alternatives.

1. You can play football in the park, but famous teams play their matches in *playgrounds / stadiums*.
2. You might go swimming in the sea, or in *a pool / an office*.
3. At a sports *station / centre* you can do lots of different sports.
4. If you play tennis or badminton, you will need a *skate / racket*.
5. Members of a sports team wear the same colour *kit / suit* when they're playing.
6. When you play cricket or baseball, you hit the ball with a *bat / fly*.
7. In a football match, the winning team is the one that gets the most *prizes / goals*.
8. If you play a sport a lot, you might join a *club / competition*.

☑ Exam task

2

Read the advertisement and the email.
Fill in the information in Felix's notes.

Kingsfield Sports Centre – open daily from 7 am to 10 pm
NEW – tennis and badminton

Tuesday or Friday only

£7 per game (£5 for students)
Call 3464 4754 to book – payment by credit card. No cash.

● ● ●   Reply   Forward

From: Cara   To: Felix

Can you book a game for us at the sports centre? I don't have a credit card. You can play on two different days, but I'm working until 9 pm on Tuesday. Book for 7 pm, and let's play badminton – it's easier than tennis! We get a discount because we're students.

Felix's Notes
Game with Cara
Name of sports centre: *Kingsfield*
Sport we'll play: **1** ....
Day we'll play: **2** ....
Time we'll start: **3** ....
Price we'll pay: **4** ....
How we'll pay: **5** ....

3 Samuel needs to complete a form to join a sports centre. Complete the form with the correct information from the box (a–h).

---

a swimming and tennis   **b** by credit card   **c** sbraun@redmail.co   **d** no

e 12   **f** Mr   **g** Station Road   **h** my mother, Stella Braun

---

Title: (1) ....
Full name: Samuel Braun
Date of birth: 15 / 07 / 1998
Flat / House number: (2) ....
Street Name: (3) ....
Post code: 16370
Phone number: 01433 45745
Email address: (4) ....

Who should we contact if you have an accident at the sports centre? **(5)** ....

What is the contact number of this person? 01433 546 858

Are you taking any medicine at the moment? **(6)** ....

How do you want to pay? **(7)** ....

Which sports are you most interested in doing here? **(8)** ....

☑ **Exam tips**

- You need to read both texts to find the five answers.
- Look at the notes and think about what kind of information you have to find for each question – for example, a date, time, place, a price, etc.
- You must use words and numbers from the texts to complete the notes.
- Make sure you copy the words and numbers correctly.

Food and drink

1a Complete the table with the words from the box.

carrot	chicken	grapes	melon	pear
pepper	potato	sausages	steak	

vegetables	fruit	meat
....	....	....
....	....	....
....	....	....

1b Add more food words you know to the table. Can you think of any dishes that you could make with some of these ingredients?

 Exam task

2 Read the advertisement and the email.

Fill in the information in Ralf's notes.

The Orange House
Excellent Italian cooking

Open Tuesday to Saturday, 11 am to 11 pm

10% discount on Tuesdays and Wednesdays

Call 0345 48234 to book

● ● ●   **Reply**   **Forward**

From: Theo   To: Ralf

About Oscar's birthday - he likes French and Italian food, so let's try that restaurant in the advertisement. His birthday is on Thursday, but we'll go on Wednesday to get the discount. There'll be six of us, because two of the people I asked can't come. Book the restaurant for 8 pm, but let's meet at 7:45 pm. It closes at 11 pm.

Ralf's Notes
Restaurant for Oscar's birthday

Number to call: *0345 48234*

Type of food: **1** ....

Day to book: **2** ....

Time to book: **3** ....

Number of people: **4** ....

Time to meet: **5** ....

3a Number the instructions from a recipe for fruit salad in the correct order.

a   Add lemon juice and sugar to the large bowl with the fruit. ....

b   Serve your fruit salad ....

c   Wash the fruit. ....

d   Mix the fruit, juice and sugar together. ....

e   Choose the fruit you want to use. ....

f   Put the fruit salad into smaller bowls. ....

g   Put the fruit you have cut into a large bowl. ....

h   Cut the fruit into small pieces. ....

3b Write the instructions for a recipe you know.

....

....

....

....

....

....

....

....

....

 Get it right!

Look at the sentences below and choose the correct one.

I get a watch and a very good necklace and many more presents.

I got a watch and a very good necklace and many more presents.

Health and exercise

1 ▶ Read the email and the reply. Complete the reply with the correct alternatives.

● ● ●   <u>Reply</u>   <u>Forward</u>

To: Richard   From: Ash

I would like to join the gym you go to. Where is it? Which activities does it offer? Can I go there with you soon?

● ● ●   <u>Reply</u>   <u>Forward</u>

Dear Ash,
The gym **(1)** *is / am* on Station Road. I usually **(2)** *taking / take* exercise classes there,
(3) *but / so* yesterday I **(4)** *use / used* the pool. There **(5)** *are / is* exercise machines too.
(6) *I'm going / I go* there tomorrow. Why **(7)** *aren't you coming / don't you come* with me?
See you soon.
Richard

2a ▶ Complete the tips about writing emails with the correct alternatives.

When you write an email to a friend, start the email with **(1)** *Dear / Fair* or **(2)** *Hey / Hi*, and then your friend's **(3)** *title / name*.
To finish your message you can write **(4)** *'best / good* wishes' or 'see you **(5)** *soon / quickly*.

2b ▶ Write a few sentences about your favourite kind of exercise.

....
....
....
....
....
....
....
....
....

3 **Your English friend Jo goes running every day. You want to go running with Jo. Write an email to Jo.**

- **say when you want to run with Jo**
- **ask what time Jo goes running**
- **offer to show Jo a nice place to go running.**

Write **25–35** words.

....

....

....

✓ **Exam facts**

- In this part, you read a short text asking you for three pieces of information.
- The text may be a message or some notes.
- You have to write the three pieces of information in a short message.

Personal identification

1 Match the definitions with the family words.

1. your mother's brother	**a** grandmother
2. your aunt's son	**b** cousin
3. your father's mother	**c** grandchild
4. your son's daughter	**d** father
5. your sister's son	**e** nephew
6. your grandfather's son	**f** uncle

2 Complete the dialogue with the information from the boxes (a–d).

a 0648 546824.

b The fifth of October, 2000.

c Elsa Merton. That's M-E-R-T-O-N.

d 116, Greenwood Road.

Librarian: You can join the library, but I need some information first. Can you tell me your full name, please?

Elsa: (1) ....

Librarian: Thank you. And where do you live, Elsa?

Elsa: (2) ....

Librarian: That's fine. Now – what's your date of birth?

Elsa: (3) ....

Librarian: OK. And finally, what's your phone number?

Elsa: (4) ....

Librarian: Thank you Elsa. Here's your card and your book. Now I'll show you around the library.

☑ Exam task

Read the email from your English friend, Maxi.

● ● ●		**Reply**	**Forward**
To:	**From: Maxi**		

I've received a wedding invitation from your brother. It's so nice of him! Can you suggest a place in your city where I can stay? What do people usually wear to weddings in your country? What can I buy them for a present?

Write an email to Maxi and answer the questions.

Write 25–35 words.

....
....
....
....
....
....
....
....
....

☑ Exam tips

- Read the instructions carefully to find out what you need to write.
- You must write all three pieces of information.
- When you finish your message, check your spelling and grammar.

Entertainment and media

1 ▶ **Complete the sentences with the words in the box.**

actor	channel	exhibition	fan
movie	screen	stage	video games

1. If you don't like the TV programme, change the ....
2. My friend is a big .... of that group. She goes to all their concerts.
3. I love playing .... online with my friends.
4. I'm going to that photography .... at the museum tomorrow.
5. Let's see that film. Your favourite .... is in it.
6. The .... at that new cinema is really big.
7. I didn't have a good seat at the theatre. I was a long way from the ....
8. Another word for a film is a ....

2 ▶ **Add the punctuation (question marks, full stops, capital letters and apostrophes) to the sentences.**

1. Id like to go to that concert

....

2. are you going to the party tonight

....

3. my friend sara is going to be in a show

....

4. this isnt carlas guitar

....

5. ive never been to the opera

....

6. i dont like that artist

....

7. i think well need to buy a ticket

....

8. do you know where i live

....

3 ▶ Your English friend Charlie has invited you to the cinema tomorrow, but you can't go.

Write an email to Charlie.

- tell Charlie that you are sorry
- explain why you can't go
- say which day you can go instead.

Write **25–35** words.

....

....

....

 Get it right!

Look at the sentence below. Then try to correct the mistake.

I'm having a day off next week I would like to come to visit you.

Services and places

1 Match the question to the answer.

1. When shall we meet?	**a** At 8:30 am every day.
2. What time does the next train leave?	**b** At 6:15 pm, outside the cinema.
3. When is your sister's birthday?	**c** At twenty to eight, on platform three.
4. What time does the post office open?	**d** In 2009. We were in the same class at school.
5. When is your doctor's appointment?	**e** Saturday. I love the weekend!
6. How long have you lived in Sydney?	**f** Next Wednesday at 1:15 pm.
7. When do you play hockey?	**g** On the 22nd September.
8. Excuse me, what's the time please?	**h** On Tuesdays, in the sports centre.
9. When did you meet your best friend?	**i** Since 2014.
10. What's your favourite day of the week?	**j** It's ten o'clock.

☑ Exam task

2 🔊 Track 5 **You will hear five short conversations.**
You will hear each conversation twice.
There is one question for each conversation.
For questions 1–5, put a tick (✓) under the right answer.

1. Where is the post office?

 A ☐   B ☐   C ☐

2. What does the man order?

 A ☐   B ☐   C ☐

3. How much does the man spend?

 A ☐   B ☐   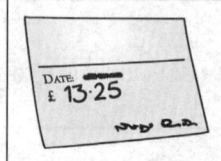 C ☐

4. Where are the girls going today?

A

B

C

5. When is the woman going to the dentist?

A

B

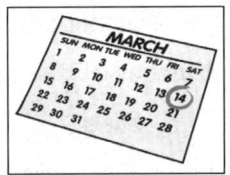
C

3

Match the words in the box to the sentences and questions.

cinema	dentist	hotel	library	museum	restaurant
sports centre	theatre	tourist information centre		train station	

1. The paintings were discovered in Italy in 1843. ....

2. Excuse me, what time does the play finish? ....

3. Can I have a return ticket to Bradford, please? ....

4. You are in room 321, on the third floor. Here is the key. Enjoy your stay. ....

5. I'll have a chicken salad, please. ....

6. Would you like a map of the city? ....

7. Good morning. I've got an appointment at 4:30. ....

8. What time does the aerobics class start? ....

9. Let's buy tickets for the new James Bond film now! ....

10. Can I borrow these books, please? ....

☑ *Exam facts*

- In this part, you listen to five short conversations.
- There are five questions with three pictures.
- You have to choose the right picture.

Shopping and numbers

1 Complete the sentences with the numbers in the box.

| eight | fifteen | seven | sixty | twelve | twenty-six | two hundred | thousand |

1. There are .... days in a week.

2. When it's 11:45, it is also a quarter to ....

3. There are a .... metres in a kilometre.

4. I'm 24 and my sister is 16. She's .... years younger than me.

5. There are .... seconds in a minute.

6. Paula lives at 16 Brick Lane and her friend lives next door at number ....

7. There are .... letters in the English alphabet.

8. Our house was built in 1793. It's over .... years old.

☑ Exam task

2 🔊 Track 6 You will hear five short conversations.
You will hear each conversation twice.
There is one question for each conversation.
For questions 1–5, put a tick (✓) under the right answer.

1. Which bus goes to the supermarket?

 A ☐   B ☐   C ☐

2. What time does the shop close?

 A ☐   B ☐   C ☐

3. Which T-shirt does the woman buy?

 A ☐   B ☐   C ☐

4. What time does the bookshop close on Saturday?

 A ☐

 B ☐

 C ☐

5. What did the man buy?

 A ☐

 B ☐

C ☐

3 Read the descriptions and complete the words. The first letter is given to you. There is one space for each letter in the word.

1. If you haven't got any cash you will need to pay with this. c _ _ _ _ _ c _ _ _

2. When you buy something the shop assistant will give you this. r _ _ _ _ _ _

3. This is a shop with many floors where you can buy lots of different things. d _ _ _ _ _ _ _ _ _
   s _ _ _ _

4. These are people who buy things in a shop. c _ _ _ _ _ _ _ _

5. There are 100 pennies in one of these. p _ _ _ _

6. You can buy food and other things in this shop. s _ _ _ _ _ _ _ _ _ _

7. You might do this before you buy new clothes. t _ _ (them) _ _

8. If you like reading, you might go to this shop. b _ _ _ _ _ _ _

9. Shoppers in America spend these. d _ _ _ _ _ _

10. When you are shopping you can ask this person for help. a _ _ _ _ _ _ _ _

☑ **Exam tips**

• Read the questions very carefully. <u>Underline</u> the most important words in the question.
• The people will talk about what you can see in all three pictures, but only one is right.
• The first time you listen, choose your answers. The second time you listen, check that your answers are right.

Education and study

1 Choose the correct alternative.

1. What time *did / does* the class finish last week?
2. Fran is always tired on Saturdays so she *got up / gets up* late.
3. *Was / Does* your mum work in a bank?
4. Max *bought / is going to buy* a new mobile phone later.
5. Kate *sends / sent* me an email two days ago.
6. *Did you / Are you going to* visit your grandmother tomorrow?
7. I sometimes *meet / am going to meet* my friends at the beach.
8. *Is / Was* Ben wearing a hat at the party last night?
9. I think *I'll go / I went* shopping tomorrow.
10. Matt usually walks home but this afternoon he is going to *ride / rides* his bike.

☑ Exam task

2 🔊 Track 7

You will hear five short conversations.
You will hear each conversation twice.
There is one question for each conversation.
For questions 1–5, put a tick (✓) under the right answer.

1. What is the boy's favourite subject?

  A ☐   B ☐   C ☐

2. Where does the girl put the dictionary?

  A ☐   B ☐   C ☐

3. What does the boy lend the girl?

  A ☐   B ☐   C ☐

4. What time does the TV programme start?

A

B

C

5. Where does the boy have lessons?

A

B

C

3 **Read about Teresa's day, then choose the correct alternative.**

> Hello. My name's Teresa. I am a teacher in a Secondary School. I usually wake up at 7:30, I have a shower and get dressed. Then I have toast for breakfast. I always listen to the news on the radio while I am having breakfast. I leave the house at 8:30 and I cycle to work. I start at 9:00 and school finishes at 4:15. After work, I often go to the pool. When I get home, I make dinner, and eat it in the living room while I watch TV. After dinner I do the washing up, walk my dog on the beach and sometimes phone my friends. I usually go to bed at 10:30. I love reading travel magazines and always look at them before I go to sleep.

1. Teresa works in a *bank / school*.
2. She has *cereal / toast* for breakfast.
3. While she is having breakfast, she listens to *music / the news*.
4. Teresa goes to work by *bike / car*.
5. She starts work at *eight thirty / nine o'clock*.
6. After work, she often *shops / swims*.
7. She watches TV while she is *cooking / eating*.
8. She eats dinner in the *living room / kitchen*.
9. She walks her dog *in the park / on the beach*.
10. She usually reads *emails / magazines* before she goes to sleep.

 Get it right!

Look at the sentences below and choose the correct one.

Next week I'm going to an interesting place near your town.

Next week, I go to an interesting place near your town.

Food and drink

1 Look at the picture and complete the questions with the words in the box. Then write the questions.

| that | these | this | those |

1. What's ....? It's milk.
2. What's ....? It's a cake.
3. What are ....? They're crisps.
4. What are ....? They're biscuits.

5. ....? They're sandwiches.
6. ....? It's cola.
7. ....? They're strawberries.
8. ....? It's water.

☑ Exam task

2 🔊 Track 8

Listen to Sarah and Mike talking about food and drink for a picnic.
What is each person going to take to the picnic?
For questions 1–5, write the letter A–H next to each person.
You will hear the conversation twice.

People		Food and drink
1 Mike	☐	A apples
2 Margaret	☐	B biscuits
3 John	☐	C cakes
4 Andrea	☐	D cola
5 Eric	☐	E hamburgers
		F ice cream
		G sandwiches
		H strawberries

3a

Write *C* (countable) or *UC* (uncountable) next to each word.

1. biscuit _ _	5. egg _ _	9. milk _ _	13. sandwich _ _
2. bread _ _	6. grape _ _	10. orange _ _	14. sausage _ _
3. crisp _ _	7. hamburger _ _	11. pasta _ _	15. sugar _ _
4. cheese _ _	8. meat _ _	12. salad _ _	16. water _ _

3b

Choose the correct alternative.

1. There isn't much *hamburgers / cheese* in the fridge.

2. There aren't many *oranges / milk* in the supermarket.

3. There are a lot of *biscuits / sugar* in our shopping basket.

4. There is a lot of *sausages / pasta* on my plate!

5. There are a few *apples / sugar* in the cupboard.

6. There is a little *eggs / bread* on the table.

7. There *is / are* a lot of salad in this sandwich!

8. There isn't *many / much* water in the bottle.

9. There are a *few / little* grapes in the bowl.

10. *Are / Is* there any crisps in the bag?

11. There aren't *many / much* sandwiches in the shop.

12. There is a *few / little* meat in the freezer.

 Exam facts

- In this part, you listen to a conversation between two people who know each other.
- You have to match two lists of information.

© Cambridge University Press and UCLES 2015

Hobbies and shopping

1

Look at the table and read the sentences. Are they TRUE or FALSE?

	Surfing	Playing computer games	Going shopping	Dancing
Agatha	✓✓	✗	✓	✗
Hugh	✓✓✓	✓	✗	✓
Vanessa	✓	✓✓	✗	✓✓✓

1. Agatha likes playing computer games. ....
2. Hugh thinks surfing is more interesting than dancing. ....
3. Vanessa prefers surfing to dancing. ....
4. Agatha enjoys surfing and dancing. ....
5. Hugh's favourite hobby is playing computer games. ....
6. Vanessa is not interested in going shopping. ....
7. Agatha doesn't like playing computer games or dancing. ....
8. Hugh thinks playing computer games is boring. ....
9. Agatha prefers going shopping to dancing. ....
10. Hugh and Vanessa don't enjoy going shopping. ....

☑ Exam task

2

🔊 Track 9

Listen to Sonia and Dan talking about shopping.
What did Sonia buy in each shop?
For questions 1–5, write the letter A–H next to each shop.
You will hear the conversation twice.

Shops
1 clothes shop ☐
2 bookshop ☐
3 supermarket ☐
4 sports shop ☐
5 market ☐

Things
A bag
B cake
C flowers
D shampoo
E socks
F towel
G trainers
H trousers

3 Choose the correct response to each question, a, b or c.

1. Can I help you?

   a Yes, please.   **b** Pleased to meet you.   **c** Good bye.

2. Could I try this on, please?

   a It's £10.   **b** Yes, of course.   **c** It's very big.

3. Would you like me to put the receipt in the bag?

   a No, thanks.   **b** That's nice.   **c** It's very heavy.

4. Should I make dinner this evening?

   a No, it's OK. I'll do it.   **b** I don't like it.   **c** I'll have a ham and cheese pizza, please.

5. Can I take your order?

   a A table for two, please.   **b** OK, thank you.   **c** Yes. Two hamburgers, please.

6. Would you carry this bag for me, please?

   a Yes, please.   **b** Yes, of course.   **c** No, I wouldn't.

7. Can I have two return tickets to Manchester, please?

   a When do you want to travel?   **b** That's fine.   **c** How much is it?

8. Shall I go to the supermarket this afternoon?

   a Yes, I like chicken.   **b** No, we will have chicken for dinner.   **c** Yes, can you buy some chicken?

9. Could you close the window, please?

   a Yes, are you cold?   **b** No, I'm cold.   **c** Yes, I'm sorry.

10. Would you like a drink?

    a No, I'm not hungry.   **b** No, thanks.   **c** Yes, an ice cream please.

4 Write four sentences about yourself. Use *enjoy / favourite / prefer ... to / don't like.*

1. ....

2. ....

3. ....

4. ....

☑ *Exam tips*

- Before you listen, read the two lists and think about what the conversation might be about.
- In the second list, the words you hear are often different from the words you read.
- You can only use an answer once. When you have used an answer, ~~cross it out~~.

Countries and sports

1 Complete the table with the correct words.

Country	Nationality	Language
(1)	Australian	English
Brazil	(2)	Portuguese
The United Kingdom	British	(3) ....
(4)	Chinese	Chinese
France	(5)	French
(6)	Mexican	Spanish
Italy	Italian	(7) ....
Turkey	(8)	Turkish

☑ **Exam task**

2

🔊 Track 10

Listen to Tanya talk to a friend about a sports camp.
Which sport did each person try?
For questions 1–5, write the letter A–H next to each person.
You will hear the conversation twice.

People

1 Chris ☐
2 Gina ☐
3 Tom ☐
4 Emma ☐
5 Harry ☐

Sports

A basketball
B climbing
C golf
D horse riding
E sailing
F swimming
G tennis
H windsurfing

3 **Put the words in the correct order to make suggestions. Use the responses to help you.**

1. don't / Why / we / on / shopping / go / Thursday / ?

....

No, I don't like shopping!

2. go / you / like / to / at / skiing / the / Would / weekend / ?

....

I'd love to, but I have to work.

3. beach / running / morning / on / the / Let's / to / tomorrow / go /.

....

Good idea!

4. want / to / Do / play / you / at / tennis / after / school / ?

....

No, sorry. I can't.

5. a / we / movie / Shall / watch / later / ?

....

OK. We can see the new Tom Cruise film.

6. walk / going / What / for / a / park / in / afternoon / about / the / this / ?

....

No, that's boring, but we could go skateboarding instead!

(◎) *Get it right!*

Look at the sentences below. Then try to correct the mistake in each one.

I like listening to musics and seeing films.

Did you get much presents?

Leisure time

1   **Match the questions and answers. Then underline the answer word(s).**

1. How much did you pay for that video game, Chris? ....
2. Was it sunny in France last week, Jane? ....
3. When do you have dance lessons, Alex? ....
4. What time does the picnic start on Sunday? ....
5. When are you going to the *One Star* concert in London? ....
6. Where did Bella learn English? ....

a   They are playing for three nights, but my ticket's for the 25th September.

b   The full price is £15, but my brother works in the computer shop and he gets a discount, so I only paid £12!

c   At about 12.00, but I'm meeting Felix at the station at 11:30 and we're going together.

d   No, it wasn't. It was cloudy, but it didn't rain!

e   Every Friday. Do you want to come next week?

f   She lived in London for two years when she was twenty.

☑ Exam task

2   📢 **Track 11 Listen to Jack talking to his friend Martin about music.**

For each question, choose the right answer (A, B or C). You will hear the conversation twice.

1 What is the name of Martin´s music teacher?

   A Harry

   B Peter

   C Steve

2 Martin has music lessons on

   A Tuesdays.

   B Thursdays.

   C Saturdays.

3 How long does Martin practise at the weekend?

   A 1 hour

   B 2 hours

   C 3 hours

4 Where is the music festival?

   A at the music school

   B in the park

   C in the shopping centre

5 Martin will start playing

   A at 6:15.

   B at 7:00.

   C at 7:45.

3a Complete the table with the words in the box.

the beach	a bike	a camera	the cinema	cooking
a fishing rod	go to a festival	go to a restaurant		have a barbecue
have a picnic	a mobile phone	a museum		painting
the park	reading	taking photos		

Favourite things	Hobbies	Places to go	Things to do at the weekend
....	....	....	....
....	....	....	....
....	....	....	....
....	....	....	....

3b Answer the questions about yourself.

1. What do you do in your free time?

....

2. Can you play an instrument?

....

3. What is your favourite thing?

....

4. Where do you usually meet your friends?

....

5. How often do you go the cinema?

....

6. What did you do yesterday afternoon?

....

7. What are you going to do at the weekend?

....

8. Have you ever been to a music festival?

....

> ☑ **Exam facts**
>
> • In this part, you listen to a conversation between two people.
> • There are five questions and you have to choose the right answer (A, B or C).
>
> © Cambridge University Press and UCLES 2015

Social media and technology

1 Put the letters in the right order to make words. Then complete the sentences.

1. I usually .... games onto my laptop computer to practise my English. (dwondaol)

2. I use my .... to call my friends, take photos and send messages. (emboil npohe)

3. You can find out about lots of things on the .... (ietrentn)

4. I often play .... in my spare time. (voied gsmae)

5. My favourite band have got an amazing .... with interesting facts and information on it. (wbe pega)

6. My sister loves taking photos with her .... (dtiliga cmraea)

7. Some people spend many hours chatting to friends .... (oinnel)

8. Q is the first letter on most .... (ekybardos)

9. You can use a .... to open and close documents on your computer. (mesuo)

10. I send lots of .... every day at work. (ealims)

☑ **Exam task**

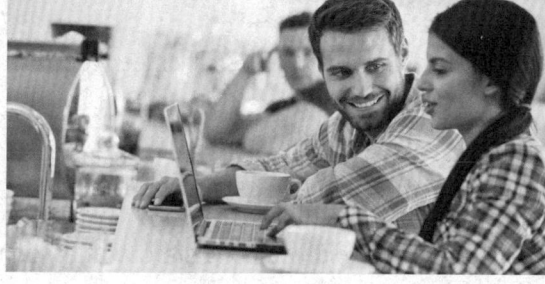

2 ◀)) Track 12 Listen to Lisa talking to her friend Robert about computers.

For each question, choose the right answer (A, B or C). You will hear the conversation twice.

1 Where did Lisa buy her laptop?
  A Bridge Street
  B Green Street
  C High Street

2 The most useful website was
  A buy_a_computer.com
  B computers_and_phones.com
  C new_laptop.com

3 Lisa's new laptop weighs
  A one kilogramme.
  B 1.5 kilogrammes.
  C two kilogrammes.

4 How much did Lisa pay for her laptop?
  A £579
  B £699
  C £849

5 Why did Lisa buy a new laptop?
  A to talk to her brother
  B to shop online
  C to study

3   **Rewrite the sentences in the past or present passive.**

1. Martin Cooper invented the first mobile phone in 1973.

....

2. Lots of people watch videos on the internet.

....

3. My brother didn't write that email.

....

4. People often read news articles online.

....

5. Tim Berners-Lee created the first website in 1991.

....

6. Young people usually play video games at home.

....

7. The teacher showed the students some useful websites.

....

☑ **Exam tips**

- You have to answer a question or complete a sentence.
- You will hear all three answers, but only one is right.
- The same person usually gives all of the answers.

> ## *Travel and holidays*

1 Complete the sentences with the words in the box. There are some words that you do not need to use.

> article   bill   comics   diary   diploma
> form   magazines   menu   newspaper   passport
> postcard   project   text book   ticket

1. My little brother loves reading ....

2. We haven't finished all the exercises in our English .... yet.

3. Great! The .... in this restaurant is in English!

4. Lots of people read fashion ....

5. I usually read the .... on the train in the morning.

6. My sister writes in her .... every day.

7. Sandra, you need to get a new .... to travel to New Zealand.

8. I always send my parents a .... when I am on holiday.

9. You must keep your .... for the return journey.

10. I read an interesting .... about sport on the internet.

☑ **Exam task**

2 ◀)) Track 13 **Listen to James talking to Susan about his holiday.**

For each question, choose the right answer (A, B or C).
You will hear the conversation twice.

1 How long is James's holiday?

  A one week

  B two weeks

  C three weeks

2 Where is James flying to first?

  A Manchester

  B Miami

  C Paris

3 Where did James go in January?

  A Canada

  B Mexico

  C The USA

4 How long is the flight to Miami?

  A five hours

  B 8.5 hours

  C 16 hours

5 The aeroplane arrives in Manchester at

  A 1:00 pm

  B 5:35 pm

  C 11:05 am

3a Match 1–10 with a–j.

1. I'm	**a** 'm flying to Mallorca tomorrow.
2. Emily and Vicky	**b** they're going to visit the Old Town tomorrow.
3. We're going	**c** are travelling around the USA this summer.
4. I'm not going to stay	**d** coming to visit us in July.
5. Tom	**e** to go swimming tomorrow.
6. My grandmother's	**f** going to take a photo of the beach now.
7. I	**g** 's going to take us to the lake after lunch.
8. My brother isn't driving	**h** lunch at half past one.
9. We're having	**i** on a campsite this year.
10. My parents love sightseeing so	**j** to France in August, he's flying.

3b Write a few sentences about your next holiday.

....
....
....
....
....
....
....
....
....
....

 Get it right!

Look at the sentence below. Then try to correct the mistake.

This present gave to me by my old German friend.

Making plans

1a Complete the sentences with the words in the box.

| autumn | birthday | century | clock | diary | evening | weekly | yesterday |

1. Today is Wednesday so .... was Tuesday.

2. The big .... on the wall in my office says it's 5:15 pm.

3. If you have a meeting every Monday, it's a .... meeting.

4. There are one hundred years in a ....

5. The book where people write their appointments is called a ....

6. .... is the season when the leaves fall from the trees.

7. People usually give you presents on your ....

8. The time between the afternoon and the night is called the ....

1b Complete the table with the words and phrases in the box.

every day	Friday morning	half past three	January	last year
Mondays	the afternoon	the moment	the weekend
tomorrow	2013	15th May

at	in	on	no preposition
....	....	....	....
....	....	....	....
....	....	....	....

☑ Exam task

2 ◀)) Track 14 **You will hear a woman talking to a customer about renting a boat.**

Listen and complete each question.
You will hear the conversation twice.

Customer information

Name: Philip Cook

Birthday: 1st December **(1)** ....

Number of people to rent boat: **(2)** ....

Pets: **(3)** ....

Dates: From 23rd August – **(4)** ....

Phone number: **(5)** ....

Read the dialogue. Choose the best word for each space, a, b or c.

Mario: Hello Tanya. Where are you **(1)** .... to go on holiday this year?

Tanya: I **(2)** .... going to go to Tenerife in August.

Mario: That sounds fun! Will it be hot?

Tanya: Yes, it **(3)** .... . I've bought a new hat and some sunglasses.

Mario: Really? Who **(4)** .... you going to go with?

Tanya: With my friends Lara and Michelle.

Mario: My sister went to Tenerife last year. She said that the beaches are amazing.

Tanya: I know. But we **(5)** .... have a lot of free time to explore the island!

Mario: Why not? What are you going to do?

Tanya: We **(6)** .... going to study Spanish in a language school.

Mario: That sounds fun. Are you going **(7)** .... lessons every day?

Tanya: Yes, we are.

Mario: Do you think you **(8)** .... be in the same class as your friends?

Tanya: No, we **(9)** .... be, because my friends speak better Spanish than me.

Mario: **(10)** .... you send me a postcard?

Tanya: Yes, of course! What's your address?

1.	**a** going	**b** doing	**c** will
2.	**a** 'm	**b** 's	**c** 'll
3.	**a** going	**b** is	**c** will
4.	**a** is	**b** are	**c** will
5.	**a** am	**b** will	**c** won't
6.	**a** 'm	**b** 're	**c** 'll
7.	**a** has	**b** have	**c** to have
8.	**a** are	**b** will	**c** is
9.	**a** aren't	**b** will	**c** won't
10.	**a** will	**b** going to	**c** are

☑ **Exam facts**

- In this part, you listen to a short conversation between two people.
- There is a form that you have to complete with words and numbers.

Health, medicine and exercise

1

Read the descriptions and complete the words. The first letter is given to you. There is one space for each letter in the word.

1. Some animals have got a big one of these, for example humans and dolphins. b _ _ _ _
2. If you have a problem with this, you go to the dentist. t _ _ _ _
3. You use these to see. e _ _ _
4. This might be curly or straight. h _ _ _
5. You wear shoes on these. f _ _ _
6. This is between your head and your body. n _ _ _
7. You have ten of these on your hands. f _ _ _ _ _ _
8. This moves your blood around your body. h _ _ _ _
9. If you eat a lot of cake, you might have a pain here. s _ _ _ _ _ _
10. Some people write with their left one of these. h _ _ _

☑ Exam task

2

🔊 Track 15 **You will hear a man telephoning a medical centre for advice.**

Listen and complete each question.
You will hear the conversation twice.

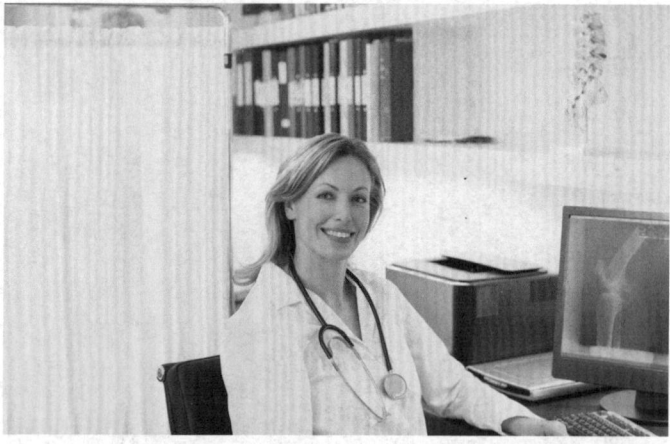

Medical advice

Address of chemist: Park Street

Cost of taxi: € **(1)** ....

Doctor's name: Doctor **(2)** ....

Time of appointment: **(3)** ....

Doctor speaks: **(4)** ....

Hospital phone number: **(5)** ....

3 **Read the conversations. Choose the correct modal verb.**

1. I've got a toothache.

   > You *might / should* go to the dentist!

2. Chris has fallen off his motorbike and now his arm hurts.

   > It *might / should* be broken so he *might not / shouldn't* move.

3. Emma fell over when she was running and has hurt her ankle.

   > I think she *might / should* put a bandage on it.

4. I've got a headache.

   > You *might / should* lie down in your bedroom and take this medicine.

5. Can you help me? I've cut my hand on a rock.

   > There is a lot of blood so you *might / should* see a doctor.

6. Lucy is very hot.

   > She *might not / shouldn't* go to school today because she *might / should* have a temperature.

7. I'm really tired and I don't feel well.

   > You *might / should* go to bed, you will feel better tomorrow.

8. Mum, I feel sick. My stomach hurts.

   > You *might not / shouldn't* eat any more sweets, Jeremy. And take some medicine.

☑ *Exam tips*

- Before you listen, read the form carefully.
- Think about what kind of information you need to write for each question – for example, a day, time, name, phone number, etc.
- You usually have to write the name of a person or place. One of the speakers will spell it.

Dates and services

1a Match the numbers to the words.

1st	fifth
2nd	first
3rd	fourteenth
4th	fourth
5th	ninth
9th	second
12th	third
13th	thirteenth
14th	thirty-first
20th	twelfth
25th	twentieth
31st	twenty-fifth

1b Complete the sentences with the words from Exercise 1a.

1. The listening paper is the .... part of the exam.
2. March is the .... month of the year.
3. *E* is the .... letter of the alphabet.
4. December is the .... month of the year.
5. Halloween is on the .... of October.
6. *M* is the .... letter of the alphabet.
7. Christmas Day is on the .... of December.
8. September is the .... month of the year.
9. Valentine's Day is on the .... of February.
10. April is the .... month of the year.
11. *T* is the .... letter of the alphabet.
12. New Year's Day is on the .... of January.

🎯 Get it right!

Look at the sentences below and choose the correct one.

It is very important to me because I will go to New Zealand tomorrow.

It is very important to me because I am going to New Zealand tomorrow.

Exam task

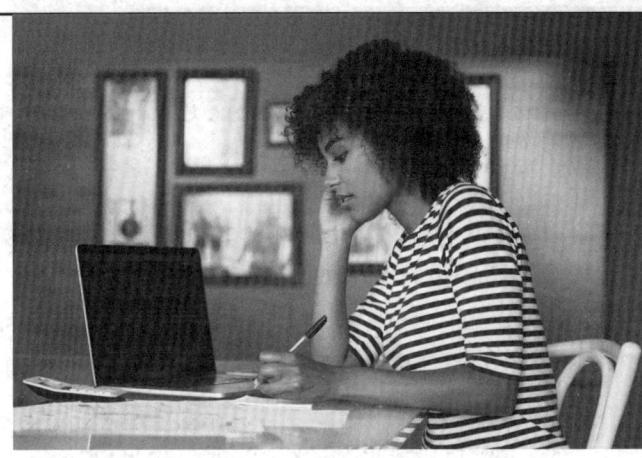

Track 16 You will hear a woman talking to a receptionist about photography lessons.

Listen and complete each question.
You will hear the conversation twice.

Photography lessons

Start: 3rd October

Classes on: **(1)** ....

Evening course costs: **(2)** £ ....

College closed in: **(3)** ....

Opening hours: Monday to Friday 9:30 am to 12:45 pm and 5:30 pm to **(4)** ....

Address: **(5)** 59 ....

3

Choose the correct response to each question, a, b or c.

1. What time does the museum close at the weekend?
   a It opens on Saturdays. **b** At half past seven.   **c** Yes, every week.

2. When is your birthday?
   a It's at five o'clock.   **b** It's in 1995.   **c** It's on the 3rd May.

3. When is your favourite programme on TV?
   a On the 6th December. **b** On Wednesday evenings.   **c** I saw it last September.

4. Do you have swimming lessons on Tuesdays?
   a No, last week.   **b** On Mondays.   **c** Yes, from seven to eight in the evening.

5. When are you going on holiday?
   a On the 13th October. **b** Yesterday, with my parents. **c** On Tuesdays from 7 pm – 9 pm.

6. What time do you get up?
   a In the morning.   **b** At a quarter past seven on weekdays. **c** It's nine o'clock in the morning.

7. When will the new video game be on sale?
   a I play it every week. **b** Last week. It was great.   **c** In the spring, I think.

8. Is the sports centre open on Sundays?
   a Yes, it opens at 9 am. **b** It's open every day from Monday to Saturday. **c** No, it closes at 5 pm.

House and home

1 Read the sentences. Choose the correct word for each space, a, b or c.

1. Can you tell me your .... please?

   a address   **b** apartment   **c** house

2. Many British houses have got .... on the floor.

   a carpet   **b** curtains   **c** downstairs

3. I haven't got a .... so I have to park my car on the street.

   a gate   **b** garage   **c** roof

4. Some people sing when they are in the .... .

   a cupboard   **b** sink   **c** shower

5. It was cold last night so I got an extra .... from the cupboard.

   a blanket   **b** pillow   **c** lamp

6. Oh no! I've lost my house .... . Can you lend me yours, please?

   a doors   **b** computers   **c** keys

7. My brother lives in a flat on the third .... of a building.

   a door   **b** floor   **c** room

8. I need to go shopping because there isn't any milk in the .... .

   a book shelves   **b** cooker   **c** fridge

9. There's a comfortable .... in my living room.

   a armchair   **b** bed   **c** television

10. Can you put a clean .... in the bathroom, please?

    a clock   **b** desk   **c** towel

☑ **Exam task**

2 🔊 Track 17 You will hear a radio programme about a house.

Listen and complete each question.
You will hear the information twice.

Matt Jackson's house

Age: 100 years old

Number of floors **(1)** ....

Hall: Photos of children and **(2)** ....

Living room: Long, green **(3)** ....

An old wooden **(4)** ....

Garden: colourful flowers and **(5)** .... trees

3 Put the words into the correct order to make questions. Then write answers about where you live.

1. Do / live / you / house / a / or / in / flat / a / ?

....

2. it / How / got / bedrooms / many / has / ?

....

3. What / door / is / your / colour / front / ?

....

4. you / a / Have / garden / got / ?

....

5. TV / you / usually / do / Where / watch / ?

....

6. you / in / got / bedroom / an / Have / armchair / your / ?

....

7. Is / in / there / a / living / your / room / clock / ?

....

8. you / Do / city / in / live / a / ?

....

☑ **Exam facts**

- In this part, you listen to one person talking.
- There is a form that you have to complete with words and numbers.

© Cambridge University Press and UCLES 2015

Entertainment and the media

1a 🔊 Track 18 **Listen and write the phone numbers.**

1. _ _ _ _ _ _ _
2. _ _ _ _ _ _ _
3. _ _ _ _ _ _ _ _
4. _ _ _ _ _ _ _
5. _ _ _ _ _ _ _

1b **Read the information and write the correct phone numbers in words.**

Emily's Language School: 4921358

Jack's Cars: 8941912

Medical Centre: 4769335

Sharps Hairdresser: 7239853

Mayfair Theatre: 6746829

1. Hello Martin, What's the phone number for the hairdresser?

It's ....

2. Can you call a taxi, please? The number is ....

3. Christina, have you got the telephone number for the English teacher?

Yes, it's ....

4. I feel sick and I think I've got a temperature.

You should call Doctor Brown on ....

5. What time does the concert finish on Saturday?

Why don't you call the ticket office and ask them? The number is ....

☑ **Exam tips**

- You will often hear two pieces of information for the same question – for example, two days, two prices, two times, etc. Listen carefully and write the right one.
- You often have to write a day of the week. Make sure you know how to spell them correctly.
- Write numbers as numbers, and not words.
- In phone numbers, for 0 we usually say 'oh'.

Exam task

2 🔊 Track 19 **You will hear a woman talking about a music festival.**

Listen and complete each question.
You will hear the information twice.

City music day

Starts: 10:30 am

All day:

Activities for children aged 6– **(1)** ....

Morning: Singing competition in **(2)** ....

First prize: A ticket for *Summer Stars* festival in **(3)** ....

Afternoon: Guitar concert

Buy tickets **(4)** ....

For more information call Jackie Webb on: **(5)** ....

3 Underline the imperatives in the sentences. Then match the people (a–j) to the sentences (1–10).

1.	Call us now to make an appointment.	**a**	a football club
2.	Phone Peter on 553442 about the next match.	**b**	a hairdresser
3.	Look on our webpage for details about the cruise.	**c**	a parent
4.	Shhh. Don't talk!	**d**	a hotel receptionist
5.	OK, everyone, show me your homework please.	**e**	a teacher
6.	Send me a postcard when you're on holiday!	**f**	a travel agents
7.	Please fill in this form before we give you your key.	**g**	a tourist information office
8.	Ask your partner some questions about the book club.	**h**	a Cambridge English Speaking examiner
9.	Paul, go to bed now!	**i**	student in a library
10.	Meet the tour guide outside the museum at 9 am.	**j**	your friend

Education and study

1 Complete the swimming pool rules with the words in the box.

POOL RULES

don't	have (x2)	must (x2)	mustn't	not	to

1. You .... follow these rules.
2. You .... run.
3. You .... have a shower before you get into the pools.
4. You must .... eat or drink in the pools.
5. If you can't swim, you .... to stay in the small pool.
6. If you have short hair, you .... have to wear a swimming hat.
7. Children under 5 years old don't .... to pay.
8. Children under 8 years old have .... be with an adult.

☑ Exam task

2 🔊 Track 20 **You will hear a teacher talking about a school trip.**

Listen and complete each question.
You will hear the information twice.

Trip to art gallery

Important information:

Wear: comfortable shoes

Arrive at school: **(1)** .... in the morning.

If you arrive late, telephone: **(2)** ....

Homework: Write about favourite: **(3)** ....

Mustn't use: Cameras or **(4)** ....

Eat lunch: **(5)** ....

3a Put the words into the correct order to make sentences.

1. You / lots / vegetables / to / of / and / eat / fruit / have / .

....

2. mustn't / in / run / corridors / You / the / !

....

3. for / You / to / take / need / this / ten / medicine / days / .

....

4. have / You / me / don't / to / help / .

....

5. your / turn / You / mobile / an / phone / in / exam / off / must / .

....

6. shout / needn't / I / You / hear / can / you / !

....

3b Read the sentences and choose the correct alternative.

1. Tom *has / must* to wear a suit to work every day.
2. We *don't have to / mustn't* touch the animals, they are dangerous!
3. Alice *must / need* speak English in the classroom!
4. Dad, you *have to / needn't* take me to the cinema, I can get the bus.
5. Jackie *doesn't have / mustn't* to go to school on Saturday mornings.
6. You *don't have / need* to call your sister this evening, she's worried about you!

 Get it right!

Look at the sentences below and choose the correct one.

You must to bring a book and a pencil case.
You have to bring a book and a pencil case.

Personal identification

1 Complete the conversation with the correct phrases.

Ben: Hello. My name's Ben. I've just moved to Newville.

Oliver: (1) ....

Ben: Hi, Oliver. Do you live in Newville?

Oliver: (2) ....

Ben: Oh, really! How often do you play sport there?

Oliver: (3) ....

Ben: What do you do at the weekend?

Oliver: (4) ....

Ben: Is there a shopping centre in Newville?

Oliver: (5) ....

Ben: And what's your favourite place in Newville?

Oliver: (6) ....

a Football and tennis but I'm not very good.

b I never shop there because I prefer to buy things online.

c I usually meet my friends to skateboard.

d Not very often. I like watching it on TV!

e Pleased to meet you. I'm Oliver.

f This park, because it's very beautiful.

g Yes, my sister goes there every Saturday.

h Yes, near the sports centre.

☑ Exam task

2 Put the words in the correct order to make questions or sentences. Ask and answer with a partner.

1. your / What's / name ?
2. surname / your / what's / And ?
3. spell / you / do / that / How ?
4. you / are / Where / from ?
5. English / your / Who / teacher / is ?
6. learning / start / English / When / you / did ?
7. get / up / time / the / you / morning / What / do / in ?
8. any / or / got / brothers / you / Have / sisters ?
9. you / to / often / do / How / music / listen ?
10. reading / like / Do / books / you ?
11. about / best / something / me / friend / Tell / your .
12. something / programme / favourite / Tell / your / me / TV / about .

3 Complete the sentences with the correct word. The first letter of each word is given to help you.

1. Bob is your first name, and Brown is your s _ _ _ _ _ _ .
2. You are a man. You are married. You have a w _ _ _ .
3. Eric has got a sister but he hasn't got any b _ _ _ _ _ _ _ .
4. Your mum has got a sister. She's your a _ _ _ .
5. My father's father is my g _ _ _ _ _ _ _ _ _ _ .
6. You've got a child. She's a girl. She's your d _ _ _ _ _ _ _ .
7. I am 15 years old and my brother is 17. We're both t _ _ _ _ _ _ _ _ .
8. Your uncle's got two children. They're your c _ _ _ _ _ _ .
9. The people who live near you are your n _ _ _ _ _ _ _ _ _ .
10. Your mum and dad are your p _ _ _ _ _ _ .

☑ **Exam facts**

- In this part, the examiner asks you questions about yourself.
- The questions are usually about your name, where you come from, your hobbies, where you study or work, etc.
- You only speak to the examiner. You don't speak to the other student.

Go to https://www.youtube.com/user/cambridgeenglishtv to watch official Cambridge English videos of *Key* and *Key for Schools* Speaking tests.

Daily life

1 Complete the conversation with the words in the box.

afternoon	evening	meeting
morning	o'clock	past	quarter
tomorrow	Tuesday	week

Matt: Hi Maria. I haven't seen you for ages! Are you going to Peter's party this **(1)** .... ? I think it starts at eight **(2)** ....

Maria: No, I have to study tonight because I've got an important maths exam **(3)** ....

Matt: Oh, okay. Good luck!

Maria: Thanks. My exams finish next week so do you want to play tennis on **(4)** .... ?

Matt: I can't. I'm **(5)** .... Martin to talk about our summer holiday.

Maria: What time are you meeting him?

Matt: At a **(6)** .... to ten. He starts work at midday.

Maria: Why don't we play tennis in the **(7)** .... ? We could meet outside the sports centre at half **(8)** .... four.

Matt: Great! But can you lend me a racket? Mine is broken.

Maria: No problem! See you next **(9)** .... and have fun at the party! Do you want me to phone you in the **(10)** .... , after my exam?

Matt: No!! I'll be sleeping!

☑ *Exam task*

2 Use the words to make complete questions or sentences. Ask and answer with a partner.

1. What | name?
2. And | what | surname?
3. How | you | spell ?
4. Who | dinner | your | house?
5. time | you | get | up?
6. Where | usually | lunch?
7. What | wear | weekend?
8. When | meet | friends?
9. Where | do | English | homework?
10. like | playing | computer | games?
11. Tell | something | last weekend.
12. Tell | something | about | favourite | sport.

3 ▶ **Put the words in the correct order to make sentences.**

1. early / never / get up / I / at / the weekend / .

....

2. reads / brother / My / comics / always / .

....

3. often / on / pizza / We / Saturdays / eat / .

....

4. is / sunny / in / It / the summer / usually / .

....

5. English / always / classes / I / on Mondays / have / .

....

6. I / tired / the evening / in / sometimes / am / .

....

7. at / I / the house / usually / leave / half past eight / .

....

8. rides / dad / a motorbike / My / sometimes / to work / .

....

9. the / never / do / cooking / I / at home / .

....

10. in / I / often / my friends / meet / the evening / .

....

☑ **Exam tips**

*   Answer with more than one word. For example, if the examiner asks you 'Where do you come from?', say 'I come from Italy' and not just 'Italy'.
*   For the last question, the examiner will ask you to speak about one thing. For example, he or she will say: 'Tell me about your family' or 'Tell me about your hobbies'.
*   Try to say three things when you answer the *Tell me about* ... question.

Go to https://www.youtube.com/user/cambridgeenglishtv to watch official Cambridge English videos of *Key* and *Key for Schools* Speaking tests.

Places and buildings

1 Choose the correct word to complete the conversation, a, b or c.

1. Have you bought your ticket to York yet?

No, but my dad is driving me to the .... to get it this afternoon.

a cinema   **b** museum   **c** bus station

2. What do you do at the weekends?

I love dancing so I always go to the .... on Fridays.

a supermarket   **b** disco   **c** theatre

3. Where do you usually meet your friends?

We often spend the whole day in the .... , but we never buy anything!

a library   **b** shopping centre   **c** park

4. Have you finished writing your postcards yet?

Yes, and now I need to buy some stamps. Where's the .... ?

a department store   **b** museum   **c** post office

5. What are you doing tomorrow afternoon?

I'm having a surfing lesson at 3 pm with my friend at the ....

a beach   **b** sports centre   **c** swimming pool

6. How often do you go to the .... ?

I usually go every Friday.

a supermarket   **b** café   **c** hotel

7. What's your favourite film?

I don't like films. I prefer watching plays at the ....

a theatre   **b** school   **c** gallery

8. Where do you do sport?

I usually go running in the .... every afternoon.

a swimming pool   **b** park   **c** shopping centre

9. Do you like reading books?

Yes, I do. I borrow books from the .... every month.

a bookshop   **b** library   **c** bank

10. Tell me about your best friend.

Her name's Rosie and she's a nurse. She works in a ....

a school   **b** pharmacy   **c** hospital

2

Complete the questions and sentences. Ask and answer with a partner.

1. What's .... name?
2. And .... your surname?
3. How do you .... that?
4. .... do you go at the weekend?
5. Where .... tourists visit in your country?
6. Is .... a swimming pool near your house?
7. How .... parks are there in your town?
8. Where do you .... shopping?
9. .... often do you watch TV?
10. What's the most beautiful place in .... town?
11. Tell me something .... your favourite place in your town.
12. .... something about your house / flat.

3

Match the questions with the answers.

1. Do you like going to the theatre? ....
2. How often do you go the cinema? ....
3. When do you usually do sport? ....
4. What do you usually do with your friends? ....
5. Where did you go yesterday afternoon? ....
6. How often do you to the library? ....
7. When do you go shopping? ....
8. How often do you watch sport on TV? ....

a Every day! I swim one kilometre every morning.

b Every Saturday! I usually go with my sister and she always buys some new clothes.

c I sometimes go there to study but I never borrow books.

d I went to the art gallery. There were a lot of tourists but I loved the paintings. Dali's were my favourite.

e Never! I always go to the stadium to watch my favourite team.

f Never, because it's very expensive. I like watching films on my computer.

g We love cooking so we usually go to the supermarket to get the food and then we make dinner together.

h Yes, I do. I love watching plays.

◎ **Get it right!**

Look at the sentence below. Then try to correct the mistake.

What time you can come?

Go to https://www.youtube.com/user/cambridgeenglishtv to watch official Cambridge English videos of *Key* and *Key for Schools* Speaking tests.

Hobbies and leisure

1 Match the questions with the answers.

1. What time do you leave the house in the morning?	**a** At home, with my family.
2. Do you wear a uniform for work?	**b** Every day, because I work in an office.
3. When do you watch TV?	**c** Some toast and a glass of orange juice.
4. What did you have for breakfast this morning?	**d** Usually around half past eight.
5. Do you listen to the radio?	**e** In the evening, after dinner.
6. Where do you usually have dinner?	**f** No, I don't. I prefer listening to my MP3 player.
7. How often do you send emails?	**g** My friends, we usually go to the gym or the swimming pool.
8. Who do you play sport with?	**h** Yes, I do, because I'm a waitress.

☑ Exam task

2 Candidate A, here is some information about painting lessons. Candidate B, you don't know anything about the painting lessons, so go to page 97 and ask A some questions about them. Now B, ask your questions about the painting lessons and A, you answer them.

Candidate A – your answers

Painting lessons

Class start: 11th January

Ten week course: £25

Our groups are very small (five people!)

"Joanna Jackson is a fantastic teacher!"

More information: ☎ 245932

Candidate A – your questions

Appleton Castle

- student's ticket £?
- buy / food?
- what / see?
- open / Sunday?
- where / castle?

Candidate B, here is some information about a castle. Candidate A, you don't know anything about the castle, so go to page 96 and ask B some questions about it. Now A, ask your questions about the castle and B, you answer them.

Candidate B – your answers

Appleton Castle

Visit us on Treetop Hill.

Enjoy our beautiful garden and museum.

Open 9:30 am – 5.30 pm (closed Sundays)

Tickets: Adults £10 Students £5

New! Buy sandwiches and drinks in our café.

Candidate B – your questions

Painting lessons

- cost?
- name / teacher?
- when / start?
- big classes?
- telephone number?

3 Put the letters in the correct order to make months and seasons.

1. Aguuts ....
2. tmuanu ....
3. Dmebeecr ....
4. Fbreruya ....
5. Jyaanru ....
6. yJlu ....
7. bSempetre ....
8. sipgrn ....
9. smuemr ....
10. rweitn ....

 Exam facts

- In this part, you talk to the other student.
- You have to read some notes and then ask and answer five questions about them.
- You only speak to the other student. You don't speak to the examiner.

Go to https://www.youtube.com/user/cambridgeenglishtv to watch official Cambridge English videos of *Key* and *Key for Schools* Speaking tests.

Sports

1 | Complete the sentences with the correct word from the box.

cycle	go	hit	kick	practise	ride	swim	throw	watch	win

1. When you play basketball, you catch the ball and .... it to the other players.
2. Next year I'm going to learn to .... a horse.
3. You have to .... the ball with a bat when you play cricket.
4. If you want to be good at sport, you have to .... every day.
5. You must be able to .... if you want to learn to surf.
6. Many people prefer to .... sport on TV at the weekend.
7. I want to .... around the city on my new bike tomorrow.
8. You mustn't .... the ball when you play volleyball.
9. I love playing tennis but I never .... my matches.
10. In the summer, I usually .... running on the beach.

☑ Exam tips

- Look at the title and picture on the card and read the notes carefully.
- Asking questions: you must ask all five questions.
- Answering questions: only use the information from your notes. Do not add any other information.
- If you don't understand what the other student says, ask him or her to say it again.

☑ Exam task

2 | **Candidate A, here is some information about a surfing competition. Candidate B, you don't know anything about the surfing competition, so go to page 99 and ask A some questions about it. Now B, ask your questions about the surfing competition, and A, you answer them.**

Candidate A – your answers

Candidate A – your questions

Surfing competition!

Saturday 15th September at 2 pm

South Beach (in front of the café)

All ages welcome!

Entry: £5 (price includes a t-shirt).

1st Prize: digital camera

Tennis lessons
- Where?
- More information?
- Advanced class / 6:15 pm?
- Every day?
- Cost?

Candidate B, here is some information about tennis lessons. Candidate A, you don't know anything about the tennis lessons, so go to page 98 and ask B some questions about them. Now A, ask your questions about the tennis lessons, and B, you answer them.

Candidate B – your answers

Tennis lessons

Make friends and get fit!

In City Park every Tuesday and Thursday

Beginners' class: 6:15–7:30 pm

Advanced class: 7:45–8:15 pm

£28.50 every month

Excellent teachers!

Find out more at www.playtennis.com

Candidate B – your questions

Surfing competition!

- for adults?
- what / win?
- where?
- when / competition?
- cost / enter?

3a Put the words in the correct order to make questions. Then read the poster and answer the questions.

1. the / Where / club / is / sports / ? ....

....

2. go / Can / in / I / June / ? ....

....

3. Fridays / Are / lessons / on / there / ? ....

....

4. find / How / I / information / can / more / ? ....

....

5. the / How / lessons / do / much / cost / ? ....

....

6. go / can / Who / to / club / the / sports / ? ....

....

Summer Sports club!

For everyone who loves sport!
Learn to play volleyball, basketball and hockey and more!
Blackstone Park
Monday–Friday 1 July to 31 August.
Lessons cost £10 for two hours.
For more information: Contact: Peter on 7532456

3b Now practise the dialogue with a partner.

Go to https://www.youtube.com/user/cambridgeenglishtv to watch official Cambridge English videos of *Key* and *Key for Schools* Speaking tests.

Travel and holidays

1a Put the words in the correct place in the table.

boat	bridge	bus stop	car	catch	drive
driver	helicopter	passenger	roundabout	taxi
tourist	traffic light	travel	visit	visitor

A thing	A person	A way to travel	A verb
....	....	....	....
....	....	....	....
....	....	....	....
....	....	....	....

1b Complete the sentences with a word from Exercise 1a. You do not need to use all the words.

1. Lots of visitors to London take a .... trip on the River Thames.
2. I took a .... ride over the Grand Canyon last year – it was fantastic.
3. Often, it is faster to .... by train than by bus.
4. I usually go to work on the bus because there's a .... at the end of my street.
5. You have to stop when a .... is red.
6. In the UK you can learn to .... when you are 17 years old.

☑ Exam task

2 Candidate A, here is some information about a day trip to a local town. Candidate B, you don't know anything about the day trip to the local town, so go to page 101 and ask A some questions about it. Now B, ask A your questions about the day trip to the local town and A, you answer them.

Candidate A – your answers

Candidate A – your questions

Day trip

Visit Bridgetown every Saturday.

Tour of old town with local guide.

Explore the castle and shop in the local market.

Hungry? Have lunch in Fin's fish restaurant!

Price: £35 (including train tickets and guided tour)

***Best Buys* Travel Agents**

- Open / Saturday?
- Expensive?
- Where?
- Phone number?
- go / USA?

Candidate B, here is some information about a travel agents. Candidate A, you don't know anything about the travel agents, so go to page 100 and ask B some questions about them. Now A, ask B your questions about the travel agents and B, you answer them.

Candidate B – your answers

Candidate B – your questions

Best Buys Travel Agents

Come and see us on Summerfield Street, Hillford.

We've got cheap holidays for you and your family!

Open 9:30 am–5 pm Monday–Friday
(Saturday: 9:30–1 pm)

New this year! Holidays in the USA and Mexico.

Tel: 6785430

Day trip

- guided tour?
- when / go?
- what / do?
- day trip / cost?
- where / eat?

---

3 ▶ **Complete the text with the correct words, a, b or c.**

My name's Joshua and I love travelling. I've been to lots places and I've **(1)** .... some amazing people. Actually, last year, I even **(2)** .... a famous actor on the beach in Mexico!

This year I've already **(3)** .... three countries. In January, I saw my sister in Spain, in March, I **(4)** .... to Italy and I've just **(5)** .... home from a holiday with my friends. It was fun but my bag **(6)** .... in the supermarket near our hotel!

This summer I **(7)** .... to California with my cousin. We **(8)** .... a motorbike along Highway One and explore San Francisco. I think we **(9)** .... an amazing time!

1. **a** have met   **b** meet   **c** met
2. **a** seen   **b** saw   **c** see
3. **a** visit   **b** visited   **c** visiting
4. **a** go   **b** gone   **c** went
5. **a** return   **b** returned   **c** returning
6. **a** stole   **b** has stolen   **c** was stolen
7. **a** am going   **b** go   **c** will go
8. **a** are going to ride **b** ride   **c** 'll ride
9. **a** had   **b** have   **c** 'll have

 Get it right!

Look at the sentences below and and choose the correct one.

Write me a letter to tell me what **are you** going to do.

Write me a letter to tell me what **you are** going to do.

Go to https://www.youtube.com/user/cambridgeenglishtv to watch official Cambridge English videos of *Key* and *Key for Schools* Speaking tests.

Think about it   Key Reading and Writing Part 1

Read about Key Reading and Writing Part 1. Are the sentences TRUE or FALSE?

1. In this part of the exam I have to match notices with the correct meaning. ....

2. All of the words in the notices will be from the Key vocabulary list. ....

3. There are two sentences for each notice. ....

4. For each question, I only need to mark the correct letter on my answer sheet. ....

5. There are eight notices in total. ....

6. I need to understand the main message of each notice. ....

7. I can use letters more than once if I need to. ....

8. There is an example at the beginning of Key Reading and Writing Part 1. ....

Think about it   Key Reading and Writing Part 2

Complete the sentences about Key Reading and Writing Part 2 with the correct alternatives.

1. There are *five / six* sentences in Part 2, not including the example.

2. *Most / All* of the sentences are about the same person, or the same subject.

3. Each sentence has a *word / two words* missing.

4. *Under / Above* each sentence there are three options; A, B and C.

5. On the answer sheet, you have to write the *missing word / the correct letter* for each question.

6. The words in Part 2 are *all / not all* on the Key vocabulary list.

7. Part 2 is a test of *grammar / vocabulary*.

8. The story makes it *more difficult / easier* to choose the correct answer.

Think about it Key Reading and Writing Part 3

Complete each sentence about Key Reading and Writing Part 3 Sections 1 and 2 with a number from the box.

| one (x2)   two   three   five (x3)   eight |

Section 1

1. There are .... short conversations in the first section of Key Reading and Writing Part 3.

2. For each question, there are .... possible answers to choose from.

Section 2

3. There is .... conversation in the second section of Key Reading and Writing Part 3.

4. The conversation is between .... people.

5. There are .... gaps in the conversation.

6. You have to complete the conversation by choosing from a total of .... sentences.

7. You only need to use .... of the sentences.

Sections 1 and 2

8. You will see .... example at the beginning of both sections of Key Reading and Writing Part 3.

 Think about it Key Reading and Writing Part 4

Complete the information about Key Reading and Writing Part 4 with the correct alternatives.

Key Reading and Writing Part 4 is a **(1)** *reading / writing* exercise. Sometimes you will be asked to read three short texts, and sometimes it is one longer text. The number of words you have to read is **(2)** *always / not always* the same. There might be **(3)** *lots of / a few words* in the text which are not in the KEY vocabulary list, **(4)** *and you will / but you won't* need to understand these words to answer the questions correctly. There are seven questions to answer, with three possible answers for each question: **(5)** *(A, B or C) / (1, 2 or 3)*.

If there is one long text to read, there are two types of multiple-choice questions:

i) Seven **(6)** *long / short* questions, each with three possible short answers.

ii) Seven short sentences about the text. You have to decide if each sentence is true, false, or if the information isn't given in the text. With this type of question, the answer will be **(7)** *don't know / not given*.

If there are three short texts to read, they will be labelled with the **(8)** *name / number* of the person in the text. You will read seven short questions and decide which text gives the answer.

Think about it Key Reading and Writing Part 5

Read the following sentences about KEY Reading and Writing Part 5. Are the sentences TRUE or FALSE?

1. Key Reading and Writing Part 5 is a writing exercise. ....

2. There are five questions to answer. ....

3. You have to choose the correct word for each gap in a text. ....

4. There are four possible answers for each gap. ....

5. The text might be information from an encyclopaedia, or a news story. ....

6. This part of the Reading and Writing exam tests vocabulary. ....

7. There is an example to help you to understand the exercise. ....

8. Example answer words are prepositions, modal verbs and conjunctions. ....

Think about it Key Reading and Writing Part 6

dictionary	first	group	line	list	sentences	spelling	verbs

Complete the sentences about Key Reading and Writing Part 6 with the words in the box.

1. Key Reading and Writing Part 6 is a test of vocabulary and ....

2. In Part 6, you have to read five short .... and write the word which each one defines.

3. The definitions are like those you can find in a ....

4. You are given the .... letter of each word to help you.

5. There is a dash (a short ....) for each missing letter.

6. The words can be nouns, ... or adjectives.

7. All of the words go together in a .... For example, words about sport, or things you find in a kitchen.

8. All of the words in Part 6 are in the Key vocabulary ....

110 THINK ABOUT IT

Think about it Key Reading and Writing Part 7

Complete the sentences about Key Reading and Writing Part 7 with the verbs in the box.

| answer | choose | fill | read | show | spell | think | write |

In Key Reading and Writing Part 7, you have to **(1)** .... a short text or two short texts, and **(2)** .... in the gaps. The texts will usually be emails, letters, or notes. If there are two texts, the second will be a response to the first. For example, the first text might be an invitation, and the second text will **(3)** .... that invitation. There are ten gaps to fill in, plus an example to **(4)** .... you what to do. There are no words to **(5)** .... from – you have to **(6)** .... of the missing word. You should **(7)** .... only one word in each gap, and you must **(8)** .... the word correctly. Part 7 tests grammar, and the missing words will usually be auxiliary verbs, modal verbs, prepositions, pronouns or determiners.

 Think about it Key Reading and Writing Part 8

Complete the sentences about Key Reading and Writing Part 8 with the words in the box.

| answers | days | diary | one | posters | price | three | spelling |

Key Reading and Writing Part 8 is a reading and writing exercise. You have to read two short texts in order to find the answers. The short texts might be emails, advertisements, **(1)** .... or notices. The part you have to complete is someone's notes or their **(2)** .... You have to find information such as times, **(3)** .... , names, etc. The answers will be one word, two words or a number (which might be a time, a date or a **(4)** .... It is very important to copy the words exactly, with the correct **(5)** .... Remember that some of the **(6)** .... will be in one of the texts, and some will be in the other text. Read both texts carefully to make sure you are writing the correct information. If you are asked for a date, for example, there may be two or **(7)** .... dates in the texts. Make sure you choose the correct **(8)** ....

Think about it Key Reading and Writing Part 9

Match the questions about Key Reading and Writing Part 9 with the answers.

1. Is Key Reading and Writing Part 9 a reading or a writing exercise?

    a The instructions will say if you should write a short letter, an email or a postcard.

2. What type of message do I write?

    b You must answer all of the questions to get full marks.

3. What information do I need to include?

    c It is a writing task.

4. What if I don't answer all the questions?

    d There will be three short questions. You should answer all of them in your piece of writing.

5. How long should my answer be?

    e You must write between 25 and 35 words.

 Think about it Key Listening Part 1

Match 1–8 with a–h to make sentences about Key Listening Part 1.

1. In Key Listening Part 1, there are

    a or a shop assistant and a customer, for example.

2. Every question has

    b between two people.

3. You have to

    c choose one answer for each question; A, B or C.

4. You will hear a conversation

    d five questions.

5. The conversations may be between friends or relatives,

    e three answer options, based on pictures.

6. You need to listen for important information, such as

    f each conversation twice.

7. You will hear

    g times, prices, days of the week or numbers.

8. You need to choose and write your answers

    h while you are listening to the conversations.

Think about it Key Listening Part 2

Complete the information about Key Listening Part 2 with the words in the box.

activities	answer	daily	eight	end	five	question	simple	twice	two

In Key Listening Part 2 you need to understand a **(1)** .... conversation between **(2)** .... people.

They might be talking about topics such as free time **(3)** .... , travel or **(4)** .... life. You will hear

the conversation **(5)** .... There are **(6)** .... questions and you have to choose from **(7)** ....

options. You should write your answers on the **(8)** .... paper while you listen and you have time at the

(9) .... of the listening test to write your answers onto the **(10)** .... sheet in pencil.

 Think about it Key Listening Part 3

Read the sentences about Key Listening Part 3 and choose the correct alternatives.

1. In Key Listening Part 3, you answer the questions by *choosing A, B or C / writing a word*.

2. You listen to *one long conversation / five short conversations*.

3. You listen to *two / four* people talking.

4. There are *five / eight* questions to answer.

5. The speakers *know / don't know* each other.

6. The speakers talk about *school, university or work / something they are interested in*.

7. You must choose *one answer / two answers* for each question.

8. You are given *one point / two points* for every correct answer.

Think about it Key Listening Part 4

Read the sentences about Key Listening Part 4. Are the answers TRUE or FALSE?

1. In Key Listening Part 4, you will hear two people talking. ....

2. The speakers will always have a British accent. ....

3. You will complete a message or notes with information. ....

4. You need to choose from A, B or C answers. ....

5. The answer will always be one word. ....

6. You can make spelling mistakes in this part of the exam. ....

7. There are five gaps to complete in a text. ....

8. The speakers might spell some of the difficult words. ....

 Think about it Key Listening Part 5

Read the paragraph about Key Listening part 5 and answer the questions.

> In Part 5 of the Key Listening test, you have to answer five questions. You will hear one person giving information about something. The information you are listening for might be a date, a time or a name, for example. The speaker might spell some words (for example the name of a street) and you must write these correctly. You need to write one or more words for each answer and you will hear the information twice. You should write on the question paper while you are listening. You will then have eight minutes to complete the answer paper at the end of the test.

1. How many questions are there in Key Listening Part 5?

2. How many speakers will there be?

3. What sort of information might you hear?

4. Will the speaker spell any words in Part 5?

5. How many words do you need to write for each answer?

6. Where do you have to write your answers while you are listening?

Think about it   Key Speaking Part 1

Read the paragraph about Key Speaking Part 1 and answer the questions with the words in the box. You do not need to use all the words.

In Key Speaking Part 1 you need to listen to the examiner and answer their questions. You will have to spell your surname and talk about yourself. For example the examiner might ask you about your interests, your town or your family. There will be another student (or maybe two) in the room too, but in this part of the speaking test you only need to talk to the examiner. There will be two examiners in the room too. One of them will talk to the students and the other one will only listen to you both. You should always try to use good vocabulary and grammar in the speaking test but it is okay to make some mistakes! Key Speaking Part 1 lasts 5–6 minutes.

five to six   nationality   no   surname   the examiner   the other student   two   yes   yourself

1. Will the examiner give you a card with questions on it? ....
2. What will you have to spell? Your ....
3. What will you talk about? ....
4. Who will you talk to? ....
5. How many speaking examiners will there be? ....
6. How long is this part of the Key exam? .... minutes

---

 Think about it   Key Speaking Part 2

Read the text. Then match the questions about the Key Speaking test Part 2 with the answers.

In the second part of the speaking test you have to talk to another student. You will have to ask and answer questions but you do not have to give personal information about yourself. The examiner will give you a card with some information on it. The information might be about daily life, hobbies or free times activities. You have to look at the card and answer the other student's questions. For example, your card might have information about a new club or a competition and your partner might ask you questions about times, places or prices on it. You have to find the answers on your card and tell the other student what they are. Later, the examiner will give you a different card and you will ask the other student some questions. This part of the test takes about three or four minutes.

1. Who do you have to talk to?
2. Do you have to give information about yourself?
3. Do you have to ask questions or answer questions?
4. What will the examiner give you?
5. How do you know what to ask your partner?
6. Where can you find the answer to your partner's questions?

a   A card with information or questions ideas on it.

b   The other student.

c   Both of them.

d   You need to use the words on your card to help you make questions.

e   No, you don't.

f   On your information card.

KEY TOPIC LISTS

Appliances

camera	DVD (player)	laptop	telephone
CD (player)	electric	lights	television / TV
cell phone	electricity	mobile (phone)	video
clock	fridge	MP3 player	washing machine
computer	gas	PC	
cooker	heating	phone	
digital camera	lamp	radio	

Clothes and Accessories

bag	fashion	raincoat	tights
bathing suit	glasses	ring	trainers
belt	glove	scarf	trousers
blouse	handbag	shirt	try on (v)
boot	hat	shoes	T-shirt
bracelet	jacket	shorts	umbrella
cap	jeans	skirt	uniform
chain	jewellery / jewelry	suit	wallet
clothes	jumper	sunglasses	watch
coat	kit	sweater	wear (v)
costume (swimming)	necklace	swimming costume	
dress	pocket	swimsuit	
earring	purse	tie	

Colours

black	golden	orange	red
blue	green	pale	white
brown	grey	pink	yellow
dark	light	purple	

Communication and Technology

address	cell phone	digital camera	file
at / @	chat	dot	information
by post	click (v)	download (n & v)	internet
call (v)	computer	DVD (player)	keyboard
camera	conversation	email (n & v)	laptop (computer)
CD (player)	digital	envelope	mobile (phone)

mouse	phone	software	web
MP3 player	photograph	talk	web page
net	photography	telephone	website
online	printer	text (n & v)	
PC	screen	video	

Documents and Texts

ad / advertisement	diary	magazine	passport
article	diploma	menu	postcard
bill	email	message	project
book	form	newspaper	text (n & v)
card	letter	note	textbook
comic	licence	notebook	ticket

Education

advanced	course	lesson	ruler
beginner	desk	level	school
biology	dictionary	library	science
blackboard	diploma	mark	student
board	eraser	maths/mathematics	studies
book	exam(ination)	note	study (v)
bookshelf	geography	physics	subject
chemistry	history	practice (n)	teach
class	homework	practise (v)	teacher
classmate	information	project	term
classroom	instructions	pupil	test (n)
clever	know	read	university
coach	language	remember	
college	learn	rubber	

Entertainment and Media

act	card	dance (n & v)	festival
actor	cartoon	dancer	film (n & v)
adventure	CD (player)	disco	fun
advertisement	chess	draw	go out
art	cinema	drawing	group
article	classical (music)	drum	guitar
board game	competition	DVD (player)	hip hop
book	concert	exhibition	instrument

keyboard	newspaper	pop (music)	sing
laugh	opera	practice (n)	singer
listen to	paint (v)	practise (v)	song
look at	painter	programme	television / TV
magazine	photograph	project	theatre
MP3 player	photographer	radio	ticket
museum	photography	read (v)	video (game)
music	piano	rock (concert)	watch (v)
musician	picture	screen (n)	
news	play (n)	show (n)	

Family and Friends

aunt	girl	group	mum(my)
boy	grandchild	guest	neighbour
brother	grand(d)ad	guy	parent
child	granddaughter	husband	pen-friend
cousin	grandfather	love (n & v)	sister
dad(dy)	grandma	married	son
daughter	grandmother	Miss	surname
family	grandpa	mother	teenager
father	grandparent	Mr	uncle
friend	grandson	Mrs	wife
friendly	granny	Ms	

Food and Drink

apple	butter	coffee	fish
bake	cafe/café	cola	food
banana	cafeteria	cook (n & v)	fork
barbecue	cake	cooker	fridge
biscuit	can (n)	cream	fried
boil	candy	cup	fruit
boiled	carrot	curry	garlic
bottle	cereal	cut (n)	glass
bowl	cheese	dessert	grape
box	chef	dinner	grilled
bread	chicken	dish (n)	honey
break (n)	chilli	drink	hungry
breakfast	chips	eat	ice
burger	chocolate	egg	ice cream

jam	mineral water	potato	sweet **(n & adj)**
juice	mushroom	rice	tea
kitchen	oil	roast **(v & adj)**	thirsty
knife	omelette	salad	toast
lemon	onion	salt	tomato
lemonade	orange	sandwich	vegetable
lunch	pasta	sauce	waiter
main course	pear	sausage	waitress
meal	pepper	slice **(n)**	wash up
meat	picnic	snack **(n)**	yog(h)urt
melon	piece of cake	soup	
menu	pizza	steak	
milk	plate	sugar	

Health, Medicine and Exercise

accident	cut **(v)**	foot	pain
ambulance	danger	hair	problem
appointment	dangerous	hand	rest **(n)**
arm	dead	head	run
baby	dentist	health	sick
back	die	hear **(v)**	soap
bandage	doctor	heart	stomach
blood	Dr	hospital	stomach ache
body	ear	hurt **(v)**	swim
brain	exercise	ill	temperature
break **(v)**	eye	leg	tired
check **(v)**	face	lie down	tooth
chemist	fall **(v)**	medicine	toothache
clean **(adj & v)**	feel **(v)**	neck	toothbrush
cold **(n)**	finger	nose	walk
comb **(n)**	fit	nurse	well **(adj)**

Hobbies and Leisure

barbecue	camp	computer	guitar
beach	camping	dance **(n & v)**	hobby
bicycle	campsite	draw	holidays
bike	CD (player)	DVD (player)	join
book	club	festival	magazine
camera	collect **(v)**	go out	member

MP3 player	musician	party	quiz
museum	paint **(n & v)**	photograph **(n & v)**	tent
music	park	picnic	video game

House and Home

address	computer	garage	refrigerator
apartment	cooker	garden	roof
armchair	cupboard	gas	room
bath(tub)	curtain	gate	safe **(adj)**
bathroom	desk	hall	shelf
bed	dining room	heating	shower
bedroom	door	home	sink
blanket	downstairs	house	sitting room
bookcase	drawer	key	sofa
bookshelf	DVD (player)	kitchen	stay **(v)**
bowl	entrance	lamp	toilet
box	flat **(n)**	light	towel
carpet	floor	live **(v)**	
chair	fridge	living room	
clock	furniture	pillow	

Measurements

centimetre / centimeter	half	litre / liter	second
	hour	metre / meter	temperature
day	kilo(gram[me])/kg	minute	week
degree	kilometre/km/ kilometer	moment	year
gram(me)		quarter	

Personal Feelings, Opinions and Experiences (adjectives)

able	bored	different	funny
afraid	boring	difficult	good
alone	brave	excellent	great
amazing	brilliant	famous	happy
angry	busy	fast	hard
bad	careful	favourite	heavy
beautiful	clear	fine	high
better	clever	free	hungry
big	cool	friendly	important

interested	pleasant	small	tired
interesting	poor	soft	unhappy
kind	pretty	sorry	useful
lovely	quick	special	well
lucky	quiet	strange	worried
married	ready	strong	wrong
modern	real	sure	young
nice	rich	sweet	
noisy	right	tall	
old	slow	terrible	

Places: Buildings

apartment (building)	college	hospital	school
bank	department store	hotel	shop
block	disco	house	sports centre
bookshop	elevator	library	stadium
bookstore	entrance	lift	supermarket
building	exit	museum	swimming pool
cafe/café	factory	office	theatre
cafeteria	flat	pharmacy	university
castle	garage	police station	
cathedral	grocery store	post office	
cinema	guest-house	railway station	

Places: Countryside

area	forest	path	sky
beach	hill	railway	village
campsite	island	rainforest	wood
farm	lake	river	
field	mountain	sea	

Places: Town and City

airport	city centre	petrol station	station
bridge	corner	playground	street
bus station	market	road	town
bus stop	motorway	roundabout	underground
car park	park	square	zoo

Services

bank	doctor	petrol station	theatre
cafe / café	garage	post office	tourist information
cafeteria	hotel	restaurant	
cinema	library	sports centre	
dentist	museum	swimming pool	

Shopping

ad / advertisement	cheque	expensive	shop
assistant	close (v)	for sale	shop assistant
bill	closed	open (v & adj)	shopper
bookshop	cost (n & v)	pay (for)	shopping
buy (v)	credit card	penny	spend
cash (n & v)	customer	pound	store
cent	department store	price	supermarket
change (n & v)	dollar	receipt	try on
cheap	euro	rent	

Sport

ball	football	riding	swimming
badminton	football player	rugby	swimming costume
baseball	game	run (v)	swimming pool
basketball	goal	sailing	swimsuit
bat	golf	sea	table tennis
bathing suit	hockey	skate (v)	team
beach	kit	skateboard (n)	tennis
bicycle	luck	ski (v)	tennis player
bike	member	skiing	throw (v)
boat	play (v)	snowboard (n)	ticket
catch (v)	player pool	snowboarding	tired
climb (v)	(n) practice	soccer	trainers
club	(n) practise	sport(s)	v / versus
coach (n)	(v) prize	sports centre	volleyball
competition	race (n & v)	stadium	walk (v)
cricket	racket	surf	watch (v)
cycling	rest (n & v)	surfboard	win (v)
enter (a competition)	ride (n & v)	surfboarding	windsurfing
fishing		swim	winner

The Natural World

air	fire	moon	spring
autumn	flower	mountain	star
beach	forest	north	summer
bee	grass	plant	tree
country	grow	rabbit	water
countryside	hill	river	west
desert	hot	sea	winter
east	ice	sky	wood
explorer	island	south	wool
field	lake	space	world

Time

afternoon	evening	morning	tonight
a.m./p.m.	half (past)	night	week
appointment	holidays	noon	weekday
autumn	hour	o'clock	weekend
birthday	January - December	past	weekly
calendar	meeting	quarter (past/to)	winter
century	midnight	second	working hours
clock	minute	spring	year
daily	moment	summer	yesterday
date	Monday - Sunday	time	
day	month	today	
diary	monthly	tomorrow	

Travel and Transport

(aero)/(air)plane	country	fly	miss (v)
airport	delay (n & v)	garage	motorbike
ambulance	delayed	helicopter	motorway
backpack	drive	journey	move
boat	driver	leave	oil
bridge	driving/driver's	left	park (v)
bus	licence	light	passenger
bus station	engine	luggage	passport
bus stop	engineer	machine	petrol
car	explorer	map	petrol station
case	far	mechanic	pilot
coach	flight	mirror	platform

railway	ship	tour guide	tyre
repair (v)	station	tourist	underground (n)
return (n & v)	stop	tourist information	visit
ride	straight on	centre	visitor
right	street	traffic	way (n)
road	suitcase	traffic light	wheel
roundabout	taxi	tram	window
sailing	ticket	travel	
seat	tour (n)	trip	

Weather

cloud	hot	sun	wet
cloudy	ice	sunny	wind
cold	rain	thunderstorm	windy
fog	snow	warm	
foggy	storm	weather	

Work and Jobs

actor	diploma	journalist	secretary
artist	doctor	king	shop assistant
boss	Dr	letter	shopper
break (n)	driver	manager	singer
business	earn	mechanic	staff
businessman	email (n & v)	meeting	student
businesswoman	engineer	message	teacher
chemist	explorer	musician	tennis player
cleaner	factory	nurse	tour guide
coach (n)	farm	occupation	uniform
company	farmer	office	waiter/ waitress
computer	footballer	painter	work
cook (n & v)	football player	photographer	worker
customer	guest	pilot	writer
dentist	guide	police officer	
desk	instructions	queen	
diary	job	receptionist	

ANSWER KEY

Reading and Writing Part 1:1

1 1 F   2 D   3 H   4 A   5 B

2a 5 always   2 sometimes
      4 usually   1 never
      3 often

2b 1 I have a weekly meeting with my boss. / I have a
        meeting with my boss weekly.
      2 My brother plays tennis once a week. / Once a
        week my brother plays tennis.
      3 Do you always have breakfast?
      4 I drive to work every day. / Every day I drive
        to work.
      5 I often visit my sister at the weekend. / Often I visit
        my sister at the weekend.
      6 I never go to bed before midnight.
      7 My family usually eats dinner at 6pm. / Usually
        my family eats dinner at 6pm.
      8 I sometimes have lunch at my desk. / Sometimes
        I have lunch at my desk. / I have lunch at my
        desk sometimes.

3a 1 What time do you usually get up?
      2 Do you get up at a different time at the
        weekend?
      3 What do you eat for breakfast?
      4 How do you get to university?
      5 What time do (your) lessons start?
      6 Where do you have lunch?
      7 How many lessons do you have / are there
        each day?
      8 What time do you get home?
      9 What do you usually do in the evening?
     10 What time do you go to bed?

3b Students' own answers.

Reading and Writing Part 1:2

1 1 b   2 c   3 a   4 c
     5 a   6 b   7 a   8 c

2 1 E   2 G   3 D   4 B   5 C

3 1 help   4 turn / go   7 sells / has
     2 would / 'd   5 Is   8 welcome
     3 near   6 Does

Reading and Writing Part 1:3

1 1 post office   5 hotel
     2 bank   6 chemist
     3 dentist   7 tourist information
     4 library   8 café

2 Bank: 4, 7
     Tourist Information Centre: 2, 3, 8
     Library: 1, 5, 6

3 1 D   2 C   3 H   4 B   5 F

Get it right!

The weather is very beautiful and **I often stay** on
the beach.

Reading and Writing Part 2:1

1 1 price   4 store   7 change
     2 cheque   5 expensive   8 close
     3 supermarket   6 customer

2 1 A   2 C   3 A   4 B   5 C

3a 1 £11.50   4 10   7 6
      2 £12   5 2   8 £4.50
      3 3   6 £4

Narrator: 🔊 **Track 1 Reading and Writing
Part 2 Worksheet 1**

Listen to the conversations and answer
the questions.

Narrator: **One**
Man: Is that everything, madam?
Woman: Yes. How much is it?
Man: Eleven pounds fifty, please.
Woman: Here you are.

Narrator: **Two**
Man: Is this price correct – fifteen pounds?
Woman: No, that's on sale. It's twelve pounds
now.
Man: Oh, great! Thanks. I'll take it.

Narrator: **Three**
Woman: How much are those pens?
Man: Two pounds each.
Woman: Thanks. I'll take three, please.
Man: Certainly.

Narrator: **Four**
Man: Excuse me – if I buy ten of these
calendars, can you give me a discount?
Woman: Yes, I think so. They cost £1.50 each,
but if you buy ten you can have them for
twelve pounds. Does that sound okay?
Man: Yes. Thank you very much.

Narrator: **Five**
Woman: Can I buy just two of these bottles
of water?
Man: I'm sorry, madam, but they're in a pack
of four. You have to buy all of them.

Narrator: **Six**
Man: Excuse me – how much is this cheese?
Woman: It's four pounds a kilo, sir. How much
would you like?
Man: Just 200 grams, please.

Narrator:	Seven
Man:	Can I help you?
Woman:	Yes. I like those plates. How much are they?
Man:	Fifteen pounds, madam.
Woman:	Each plate?
Man:	No – that's the price for a set of six.
Woman:	Oh, that's great. I'll have those.
Narrator:	Eight
Woman:	How much did that book cost?
Man:	Four pounds fifty. But I've just seen it cheaper in a different shop. You can buy it for three pounds!

3b Students' own answers.

Reading and Writing Part 2:2

1a

1 soup	4 Coffee	7 jam
2 cereal	5 grilled	8 eggs
3 yogurt	6 ham	

1b Students' own answers.

2 1 A   2 C   3 A   4 B   5 B

3 1 C   2 W   3 W   4 C   5 C
     6 W   7 C   8 C

Reading and Writing Part 2:3

1

Group 1 Colour	Group 2 Size	Group 3 Shape
golden	large	round
purple	small	square
pale pink		star

2 1 B   2 C   3 A   4 B   5 C

Get it right!
Today we went to visit the Tower and last night we had a nice meal **at** my friend's house.

3a

1 True	4 True	7 True
2 False	5 False	8 True
3 False	6 False	

3b Students' own answers.

Reading and Writing Part 3:1

1

1 Who	4 Which	7 Where
2 How often	5 How long	8 When
3 Whose	6 What	

2 1 B   2 C   3 A   4 C   5 B
     6 E   7 H   8 G   9 B   10 A

3 Polite responses: 2, 3

Reading and Writing Part 3:2

1 1 I have never been to Japan.
     2 She has worked here for three years.
     3 Have you ever climbed a mountain?
     4 I have just seen your mum.
     5 Has the film started yet?
     6 I have already finished my dinner.
     7 We have lived here for two months.
     8 I have always wanted to meet him!

2 1 A   2 B   3 C   4 C   5 B
     6 G   7 F   8 H   9 C   10 B

3

1 Saturday	5 no
2 no	6 burgers
3 yes	7 jeans
4 8 / eight (o'clock)	8 (the) woman's (laptop)

Narrator:	🔊 **Track 2 Reading and Writing Part 3 Worksheet 2**
	Listen to the conversations and answer the questions.
Narrator:	**One**
Man:	Shall we go shopping on Friday or Saturday?
Woman:	Saturday's better. I'm meeting a friend on Friday.
Narrator:	**Two**
Woman:	I really like travelling by train.
Man:	Train! Oh no, I prefer driving!
Narrator:	**Three**
Woman:	Are you pleased with your new phone?
Man:	Sure. It's much better than the old one!
Narrator:	**Four**
Man:	We need to leave at 8 o'clock.
Woman:	Maybe we should go earlier – at 7.30.
Man:	I'm sure eight is fine.
Woman:	Oh, okay then.
Narrator:	**Five**
Woman:	That film was terrible!
Man:	Oh. I really enjoyed it!
Narrator:	**Six**
Man:	Shall we get some pizza?
Woman:	I prefer burgers to pizza.
Man:	Okay then. I'll have the same.
Narrator:	**Seven**
Man:	I don't know if I should wear a suit for the party.
Woman:	I don't think anyone else will wear a suit. Just go in jeans!

Man:	Yeah, you're probably right.
Narrator:	**Eight**
Woman:	Is that a new laptop?
Man:	Yes. But it's not as good as yours!

Reading and Writing Part 3:3

1 1 films
2 play
3 camera
4 cooking
5 meal
6 museum
7 video
8 instrument

2 1 C   2 A   3 B   4 C   5 A
6 G   7 H   8 A   9 B   10 F

3 1 mind
2 quite
3 more
4 really
5 much
6 favourite
7 like
8 even

Get it right!

There are lots of things to see here, and **I've already seen** the Statue of Liberty and the American Museum of Natural History.

Reading and Writing Part 4:1

1 1 lake
2 forest
3 island
4 plants
5 desert
6 river
7 field
8 mountains

2 1 C   2 B   3 A   4 B   5 A
6 C   7 B

3 1 e   2 b   3 d   4 f   5 a   6 c

Reading and Writing Part 4:2

1 1 languages
2 biology
3 chemistry
4 physics
5 history
6 geography
7 mathematics
8 medicine

2 1 A   2 C   3 B   4 B
5 C   6 A   7 B

3 1 broke   2 know   3 rode   4 lay
5 took   6 gave   7 see   8 go

Reading and Writing Part 4:3

1 1 passport
2 luggage
3 airport
4 miss
5 seat
6 delay
7 passengers
8 pilot

2 1 C   2 A   3 C   4 A   5 B
6 B   7 A

3 1 True   5 False
2 False   6 False
3 False   7 True
4 True   8 True

Narrator:	🔊 **Track 3 Reading and Writing Part 4 Worksheet 3**
	Listen to the conversations. Are the sentences TRUE or FALSE?
Narrator:	**One**
Woman:	Which way do I need to drive to get to the airport from here? Is it north or south?
Man:	It's north of here – about thirty minutes on the motorway.
Narrator:	**Two**
Man:	Which road do I need to take off the roundabout?
Woman:	The first turning – go left.
Man:	Not straight on?
Woman:	No – I've already told you!
Narrator:	**Three**
Woman:	Excuse me, are there any restaurants near this hotel?
Man:	Yes, madam. There's one just across the road.
Narrator:	**Four**
Woman:	If I keep going down here, will I come to the beach?
Man:	Well, yes, but it's quicker to turn left here and then first right.
Narrator:	**Five**
Man:	Which way do we need to turn?
Woman:	Well, at the moment we're going south, and we need to go west, so turn right.
Narrator:	**Six**
Woman:	The map shows the market down here on the left, but I can't see it!
Man:	That's because you're looking at the map wrong! It's actually the other way – behind us!
Narrator:	**Seven**
Man:	Excuse me – where's the George Hotel?
Woman:	Just go along this road to the end and you'll see it there in front of you.
Narrator:	**Eight**
Woman:	Is your road the second on the right?
Man:	Actually, it's the first. Quick – it's just here!

Get it right!

I **saw** my brother yesterday.

Reading and Writing Part 5:1

1a

go	play	do
swimming	football	exercise
fishing	golf	karate
skiing	tennis	Other
Other examples:	chess	examples:
cycling,	Other examples:	jazz dance,
climbing,	badminton,	gymnastics
horse riding,	baseball,	
sailing, skating,	basketball,	
skateboarding,	cricket,	
snowboarding,	hockey, rugby,	
surfing, walking,	table tennis,	
windsurfing	volleyball	

1b *Go* is used for sports which have a name ending in *-ing*.

Play is used for sports or games where you play against someone or against another team.

Do is used for all other sports and games.

2 1 C   2 B   3 A   4 C   5 A
6 B   7 B   8 A

3a 1 was cycling; saw
2 was playing
3 called; were you doing
4 were already playing
5 were playing; stopped
6 Did you go
7 forgot; lent
8 met; was fishing

3b Students' own answers.

Reading and Writing Part 5:2

1 1 c   2 d   3 g   4 e
5 a   6 h   7 b   8 f

2 1 B   2 A   3 A   4 C
5 B   6 C   7 B   8 A

3 1 B; C   2 A; B   3 B; C   4 A; C
5 A; C   6 A; B   7 A; C   8 A; C

Reading and Writing Part 5:3

1a

adjective	comparative	superlative
big	bigger	biggest
bad	worse	worst
fast	faster	fastest
dirty	dirtier	dirtiest
modern	more modern	most modern
healthy	healthier	healthiest
popular	more popular	most popular
crowded	more crowded	most crowded

1b 1 worse
2 dirtier
3 most crowded
4 healthier
5 bigger
6 popular
7 fastest
8 modern

2 1 C   2 A   3 C   4 A
5 B   6 B   7 A   8 C

3a a 3   b 4   c 1   d 5   e 2

3b Students' own answers

Get it right!

The thing I like most about it is the camera.

Reading and Writing Part 6:1

1

/eɪ/	/iː/	/e/	/aɪ/	/oʊ/	/uː/	/ɑː/
a	b	f	i	o	q	r
h	c	l	y		u	
j	d	m			w	
k	e	n				
	g	s				
	p	x				
	t	z				
	v					

2 1 clouds
2 ice
3 foggy
4 dry
5 storm

3a 1 b   2 d   3 e   4 f   5 a   6 c

3b Students' own answers

Reading and Writing Part 6:2

1

feet	head	legs
boots	hat	tights
shoes	cap	trousers
trainers		shorts

2 1 sweater
2 gloves
3 skirt
4 belt
5 scarf

3a 1 yours
2 Who
3 herself
4 someone
5 one
6 many

3b Students' own answers

Reading and Writing Part 6:3

1 1 True   2 False   3 False   4 True   5 True

2 1 short
2 pretty
3 strong
4 young
5 slim

3a 1 N 2 P 3 P 4 N 5 P 6 P

3b Students' own answers

Get it right!
Thank you for inviting **me** for a meal.

Reading and Writing Part 7:1

1 1 take 4 is 7 needs
2 walk 5 have 8 want
3 work 6 closes

2 1 in 6 been
2 What 7 because / as
3 Have 8 to
4 Do 9 will / can / could
5 When / If 10 the / this

3a 1 what 4 When 7 them
2 because 5 for 8 but
3 at 6 there

3b Students' own answers

Reading and Writing Part 7:2

1 1 may 4 might 7 Shall
2 Can 5 Would 8 mustn't
3 should 6 couldn't

2a 1 haven't seen 5 are you still studying
2 are you doing 6 'm / am doing
3 'm / am visiting 7 'm / am working
4 's / has lived 8 want

2b Students' own answers

3 1 like 5 me / us 9 do
2 have 6 for 10 because / as
3 one 7 ago
4 so 8 Is

Reading and Writing Part 7:3

1 1 went 2 drove 3 was 4 saw
5 had 6 got 7 spent 8 ate

2 1 to
2 who
3 should / can / might / will / may / could
4 which / that
5 for / about
6 the
7 did
8 your
9 if / that
10 with

3 1 Where are you going on holiday this year?
2 We need to be at the airport by ten.

3 Next year I would like to go to Germany. / I would like to go to Germany next year.
4 How are you getting to the airport?
5 I am going to China with my family.
6 How long will you stay there?
7 We are going to stay in a small hotel.
8 Are you going travelling by yourself?

Get it right!
Now **I'm writing** a postcard to you and then I'm going to lunch at the new restaurant on the beach.

Reading and Writing Part 8:1

1 1 f 2 c 3 b 4 g
5 d 6 a 7 h 8 e

2 1 Highstep (Dance School)
2 advanced
3 2 / two
4 September 3rd
5 £30

3a 1 True 5 False
2 False 6 True
3 False 7 True
4 True 8 False

Narrator: **Track 4 Reading and Writing Part 8 Worksheet 1**

Listen to the conversations. Are the sentences TRUE or FALSE?

Narrator: One
Man: I can't wait for the weekend. I'm going to the beach!
Woman: Oh, that's such a great thing to do on a sunny day.

Narrator: Two
Woman: How's the art club going, Sam?
Man: Not great! I don't know if I'll ever find a hobby I actually enjoy!

Narrator: Three
Woman: Would you like to come dancing with us on Saturday?
Man: I don't think so. It's not one of my favourite activities!

Narrator: Four
Man: Are you going on holiday this year, Amber?
Woman: Unfortunately, I'm not.

Narrator: Five
Man: Shall we go camping?
Woman: Do we have to? Isn't there a hotel?

Narrator:	**Six**
Woman:	Shall I have a party for my birthday?
Man:	Sure! Everyone loves a party – especially me!
Narrator:	**Seven**
Woman:	Shall we have a picnic on the beach?
Man:	I think I'd rather have a barbecue than a picnic.
Narrator:	**Eight**
Man:	Shall I take some photos?
Woman:	Ok, but not of me – I hate seeing myself in pictures!

3b Students' own answers

Reading and Writing Part 8:2

1 1 stadiums   4 racket   7 goals
2 pool   5 kit   8 club
3 centre   6 bat

2 1 badminton   2 Friday   3 7 pm
4 £5   5 credit card

3 1 f   2 e   3 g   4 c
5 h   6 d   7 b   8 a

Reading and Writing Part 8:3

1a

vegetables	fruit	meat
carrot	grapes	steak
potato	melon	sausages
pepper	pear	chicken

1b Students' own answers

2 1 Italian   4 six / 6
2 Wednesday   5 7:45 pm
3 8 pm

3a a 5   b 8   c 2   d 6
e 1   f 7   g 4   h 3

3b Students' own answers

Get it right!
I got a watch and a very good necklace and many more presents.

Reading and Writing Part 9:1

1 1 is   5 are
2 take   6 I'm going
3 but   7 don't you come
4 used

2a 1 Dear   2 Hi   3 name   4 best   5 soon

2b Students' own answers

3 *Sample answer*
Dear Jo,
I want to go running with you tomorrow. Is that okay? What time do you go running? I know a nice park where we can go. I can show you.
Best wishes,
Erik

Reading and Writing Part 9:2

1 1 f   2 b   3 a   4 c   5 e   6 d

2 1 c   2 d   3 b   4 a

3 *Sample answer*
Dear Maxi,
Why don't you stay with me? Men usually wear suits to weddings, and women wear dresses. They're buying a new house, so anything for the house is fine for a present.
Best wishes,
(student's name)

Reading and Writing Part 9:3

1 1 channel   5 actor
2 fan   6 screen
3 video games   7 stage
4 exhibition   8 movie

2 1 I'd like to go to that concert.
2 Are you going to the party tonight?
3 My friend Sara is going to be in a show.
4 This isn't Carla's guitar.
5 I've never been to the opera.
6 I don't like that artist.
7 I think we'll need to buy a ticket.
8 Do you know where I live?

3 *Sample answer*
Dear Charlie,
I'm sorry but I can't go to the cinema with you tomorrow because I have to study. I can go on Saturday. Are you free then?
See you soon,
(student's name)

Get it right!
I'm having a day off next week **and** I would like to come to visit you.

Listening Part 1:1

1 1 b   2 c   3 g   4 a   5 f
6 i   7 h   8 j   9 d   10 e

2 1 B   2 A   3 C   4 B   5 A

Narrator: 🔊 **Track 5 Listening Part 1 Worksheet 1**

You will hear five short conversations. You will hear each conversation twice. There is one question for each conversation.
For questions one to five, put a tick under the right answer.

Narrator: **1 Where is the post office?**

Man: Excuse me, is there a post office near here?

Woman: Yes, There's a big post office on School Street. There's a fantastic little café next to it.
You can take bus number 12 from outside the bank.

Man: Can I walk to the post office?

Woman: Yes. You have to walk through the park and turn left after the museum.

Narrator: Now listen again.

Narrator: **2 What does the man order?**

Waitress: Good evening. Welcome to The Little Italy Restaurant. Here's the menu. Would you like some garlic bread to start?

Man: No thanks. Actually, can I order now? I'd like a pizza please.

Waitress: OK and what would you like to drink?

Man: Water's fine, but could I have some salad too, please?

Narrator: Now listen again.

Narrator: **3 How much does the man spend?**

Man: Hello. Can I have two tickets for the new Pixar film which starts at 8:30, please?

Woman: Yes, of course. Are you students? Student tickets are £5.75 and you get a free drink too.

Man: I am, but my sister isn't.

Woman: OK that's £13.25 please. Adult tickets are £7.50 at the weekend.

Narrator: Now listen again.

Narrator: **4 Where are the girls going today?**

Girl 1: Hi Maya. What shall we do this afternoon? Why don't we go to the beach?

Girl 2: No! It's really cold, so we can't go swimming.

Girl 1: We could go to the museum instead. Jamie said it was fantastic.

Girl 2: OK. Then we can swim at the sports centre tomorrow.

Narrator: Now listen again.

Narrator: **5 When is the woman going to the dentist?**

Man: Good morning. Birch Street Dentists.

Woman: Hi. Can I make an appointment to see the dentist in the afternoon please?

Man: OK.I can give you an appointment at three o'clock on the 14th of March or, if you want to come in the morning she can see you at 10 am on Thursday the 12th.

Woman: Oh. I'm going on holiday on the 13th. So can I have the morning one please?

Man: OK, See you next Thursday.

Narrator: Now listen again.

3 1 museum
2 theatre
3 train station
4 hotel
5 restaurant
6 tourist information centre
7 dentist
8 sports centre
9 cinema
10 library

Listening Part 1:2

1 1 seven 5 sixty
2 twelve 6 fifteen
3 thousand 7 twenty six
4 eight 8 two hundred

2 1 B 2 B 3 B 4 A 5 C

Narrator: 🔊 **Track 6 Listening Part 1 Worksheet 2**

You will hear five short conversations. You will hear each conversation twice. There is one question for each conversation.
For questions one to five, put a tick under the right answer.

Narrator: **1 Which bus goes to the supermarket?**

Man: Sandra, do you know which bus goes to the supermarket? Is it number 23?

Sandra: I don't know. I'll have a look on their website …well, it says you need to catch bus 33 and it takes 13 minutes. The next one is at 4:30.

Man: Great. It's twenty past now. If I hurry, I'll catch it!

Sandra: OK. Bye!

Narrator: Now listen again.

Narrator:	**2 What time does the shop close?**
Man:	Oh no! We haven't got any milk! Tom, can you go to the shop, please?
Boy:	Yes, but it's half past five now. What time does it close?
Man:	At six on Saturday but it's a 15-minute walk, so you'll have to go now.
Boy:	Right. I'll put my shoes on! Shall I buy some more bread too?
Narrator:	Now listen again.
Narrator:	**3 Which T-shirt does the woman buy?**
Man:	Look at these T-shirts, Joanne. Do you like them?
Woman:	The white one's nice and the black one is OK too, but I don't like the grey one.
Man:	Really? I love the grey one and it only costs ten pounds. But I like the black one too. How much is it?
Woman:	Only eight pounds! I'll get that one! It's the cheapest!
Narrator:	Now listen again.
Narrator:	**4 What time does the bookshop close on Saturday?**
Man 1:	Good morning. Is the bookshop open at the weekend?
Man 2:	It is on Saturdays, but we're closed on Sundays.
Man 1:	Are you open all day on Saturday?
Man 2:	Yes, but we don't open until ten. On weekdays it's 9:30, but we close at eight every night.
Narrator:	Now listen again.
Narrator:	**5 What did the man buy?**
Woman:	Have you been shopping Graham?
Graham:	Yes. I went to the shopping centre with Nicola. She bought a new mobile phone. Her old phone was stolen last week on the beach.
Woman:	What did you buy?
Graham:	I only bought a computer magazine! I wanted to buy a camera for my holiday but they were too expensive.
Narrator:	Now listen again.

3
1 credit card
2 receipt
3 department store
4 customers
5 pound
6 supermarket
7 try (them) on
8 bookshop
9 dollars
10 assistant

Listening Part 1:3

1
1 did
2 gets up
3 Does
4 is going to buy
5 sent
6 Are you going to
7 meet
8 Was
9 I'll go
10 ride

2 1 A   2 A   3 C   4 B   5 B

Narrator:	🔊 **Track 7 Listening Part 1 Worksheet 3**
	You will hear five short conversations. You will hear each conversation twice. There is one question for each conversation. For questions one to five, put a tick under the right answer.
Narrator:	**1 What is the boy's favourite subject?**
Girl:	Harry, Can you help me to study for my Maths test, please?
Harry:	Of course, but I need to finish my Geography homework first.
Girl:	Thanks. I've got to do a chemistry project too! I don't like Chemistry.
Harry:	Really? I love it. It's my favourite subject.
Narrator:	Now listen again.
Narrator:	**2 Where does the girl put the dictionary?**
Teacher:	OK. Everyone put your books in your bag or under your desks. We're going to do a vocabulary test.
Girl:	Shall I put this dictionary on the bookshelf? It's not mine, it belongs to the school.
Teacher:	No, can you leave it on that table near the door please?
Girl:	OK.
Narrator:	Now listen again.
Narrator:	**3 What does the boy lend the girl?**
Boy:	Hi Josie. Have you got your English book today?
Josie:	Yes, I have. I put it in my bag last night and I've got my pencil case too... but I've left my ruler at home!
Boy:	Oh Josie! You always forget something! Do you want to borrow mine?
Josie:	Yes please. I need it for the Maths test today.
Narrator:	Now listen again.

Narrator:	**4 What time does the TV programme start?**
Mum:	There's a programme on TV tomorrow that might be useful for your history project, Melissa.
Girl:	Really? What time is it on? I've got volleyball practice at 5:45 and the coach told us not to be late!
Mum:	It's on channel 10 at five thirty. It's only half an hour long.
Girl:	I'll probably watch it online later.
Narrator:	Now listen again.
Narrator:	**5 Where does the boy have lessons?**
Woman:	Hello Patrick. Are you enjoying your university course?
Patrick:	Yes, I am. Medicine is very interesting and I love living in the city. And there's a fantastic library near my flat. I usually study there at the weekends because I have a lot of exams!
Woman:	Do you have lessons in the hospital?
Patrick:	No, we spend a lot of time there every week but all of our classes are in the main university building with the other students.
Narrator:	Now listen again.

3

1	school	6	swims
2	toast	7	eating
3	the news	8	living room
4	bike	9	on the beach
5	nine o'clock	10	magazines

Get it right!

Next week I'm going to an interesting place near your town.

Listening Part 2:1

1

1	this	5	What are these?
2	that	6	What's that?
3	these	7	What are those?
4	those	8	What's this?

2 1 F   2 C   3 B   4 A   5 D

Narrator:	🔊 **Track 8 Listening Part 2 Worksheet 1**
	Look at part two. Listen to Sarah and Mike talking about food and drink for a picnic. What is each person going to take to the picnic? For questions 1–5 write the letter A–H next to each person. You will hear the conversation twice.

Sarah:	Hi Mike. It's Sarah. I'm phoning you about the food and drink for Samantha's birthday picnic on Saturday.
Mike:	Hi Sarah. That's good. What shall I bring?
Sarah:	Well, I'm going to make some sandwiches. Why don't you bring some crisps?
Mike:	Maybe I could bring some ice cream instead? Everyone likes it and I think it's going to be very hot this weekend.
Sarah:	Good idea! Can you bring chocolate? It's my favourite!
Mike:	Sure. How many people are coming?
Sarah:	There are going to be eight of us, including Sam. Margaret has already made some cakes. They're amazing – they look like little hamburgers!
Mike:	Cool! Sam loves hamburgers.
Sarah:	John wanted to make some biscuits but he's been really busy this week so I think he's going to buy some.
Mike:	Wow! We aren't going to be hungry! Is Phil coming?
Sarah:	No. He's going to a pizza restaurant with his volleyball team.
Mike:	What about Andrea?
Sarah:	Yes. She's going to bring some fruit from her dad's garden. He's got lots of apple trees.
Mike:	Excellent! I think her dad grows strawberries too.
Sarah:	Yes, but she told me that they've already eaten them all!
Mike:	Oh no! Is anyone bringing drinks?
Sarah:	Well, we can get some water from the café in the park and I think Eric is bringing some cola from his mum's shop.
Mike:	Cool! Shall I bring my MP3 player so we can listen to music?
Sarah:	Good idea. It's going to be great!
Mike:	Yes! See you on Saturday.
Narrator:	Now listen again.

3a

1	C	5	C	9	UC	13	C
2	UC	6	C	10	C	14	C
3	C	7	C	11	UC	15	UC
4	UC	8	UC	12	UC	16	UC

3b

1	cheese	7	is
2	oranges	8	much
3	biscuits	9	few
4	pasta	10	Are
5	apples	11	many
6	bread	12	little

Listening Part 2:2

1
1	False	6	True
2	True	7	True
3	False	8	False
4	False	9	True
5	False	10	True

2 1 G   2 B   3 A   4 E   5 C

Narrator: 🔊 **Track 9 Listening Part 2 Worksheet 2**

Listen to Sonia and Dan talking about shopping.
What did Sonia buy in each shop?
For questions 1–5 write the letter A–H next to each shop.
You will hear the conversation twice.

Dan: Hello Sonia. How are you?

Sonia: Tired! I've just been to the shopping centre.

Dan: You have a lot of bags! Let me help you. What did you buy?

Sonia: Lots of things! First of all I went to the chemists and bought some more of the shampoo that I like. Then I went to Fashion World.

Dan: Of course! Your favourite shop. What clothes did you buy today?

Sonia: Actually, I bought these trainers. I want to wear them with the black trousers that I bought last week.

Dan: Very nice!

Sonia: Then I went to the bookshop. I had a drink and I bought some cake. I wanted to buy a diary for my holiday, but I forgot!

Dan: Oh dear. Did you buy anything else for your holiday?

Sonia: Yes. I went to the supermarket to look for a towel for the beach, but I didn't buy one. I bought this bag instead. Do you like it?

Dan: Yes, it's cool! Did you remember to buy something for your dad's birthday?

Sonia: Yes, I did. I bought him a present from the sports shop. He really likes football socks, so I bought him five pairs!

Dan: (laughs) Wow! Did you buy anything from the market for dinner tomorrow?

Sonia: No, I didn't. But I bought some flowers for Mum; she loves the pink ones that they sell there. I'll buy some fish tomorrow morning.

Dan: You've had a busy day!

Sonia: I know. My feet hurt and I've spent lots of money, but I've had a great time!

Narrator: Now listen again.

3
1	a	2	b	3	a	4	a	5	c
6	b	7	a	8	c	9	a	10	b

4 Students' own answers

Listening Part 2:3

1
1	Australia	5	French
2	Brazilian	6	Mexico
3	English	7	Italian
4	China	8	Turkish

2 1 H   2 F   3 G   4 D   5 A

Narrator: 🔊 **Track 10 Listening Part 2 Worksheet 3**

Listen to Tanya talk to a friend about a sports camp.
Which sport did each person try?
For questions 1–5 write the letter A–H next to each person.
You will hear the conversation twice.

Eric: Hi Tanya. Did you have good time at the sports camp in Wales last weekend?

Tanya: Yes, thank you. I went with all my friends and there were university students from other countries too. We had a fantastic time!

Eric: Really? What sports did you try?

Tanya: I went climbing! It was fun but I wasn't very good.

Eric: What about Chris? He loves water sports. Did he go sailing again?

Tanya: No, this year he learnt to windsurf, but it wasn't very windy so he didn't enjoy it.

Eric: And what about Gina? What sport did she play?

Tanya: Well, she went to the pool every morning before breakfast. The teacher was fantastic and her swimming really improved. Next year she's going to play water polo!

Eric: That's great news! And what did Tom do?

Tanya: He wanted to play golf, but the teacher was ill so he had tennis lessons instead. There were lots of people on the courts so he had fun!

Eric:	Did Emma go to the camp? She doesn't like sports.
Tanya:	That's true, but she loves animals. She went horse riding on the beach every day. Her horse was called Thunder. He was beautiful and he ran really fast!
Eric:	And did Harry play football?
Tanya:	No. Football is his favourite sport but this time he played basketball. He entered a competition with his team and they won first prize!
Eric:	He's very good at sport. He always wins competitions.
Tanya:	Yes, but he didn't win the competition on Sunday afternoon!
Eric:	Why not?
Tanya:	We were all very tired so we left the camp before lunch. He didn't play!
Narrator:	Now listen again.

3 1 Why don't we go shopping on Thursday?
2 Would you like to go skiing at the weekend?
3 Let's go running on the beach tomorrow morning.
4 Do you want to play tennis after school?
5 Shall we watch a movie later?
6 What about going for a walk in the park this afternoon?

Get it right!
I like listening to **music** and seeing films.
Did you get **many** presents?

Listening Part 3:1

1 1 b; £12
2 d; No, it wasn't.
3 e; Every Friday.
4 c; At about 12.00.
5 a; the 25th September
6 f; London

2 1 B   2 A   3 C   4 B   5 C

Narrator: 🔊	**Track 11 Listening Part 3 Worksheet 1**
	Listen to Jack talking to his friend Martin about music. For each question, choose the right answer, A, B or C. You will hear the conversation twice. Look at questions 1–5 now. You have twenty seconds. Now listen to the conversation.

Jack:	Hi Martin, Have you heard the new 'Sunny Days' song? I love the drums!
Martin:	Yeah, it's great! My brother has already learnt to play it on the piano and he knows all the words too! I'm learning to play it in my guitar class.
Jack:	Cool! I've got an old guitar at home, but I can't play it!
Martin:	You should learn, Jack! I love it! I go to classes in the Old Music School with Steve from football. We're in the same class. Our teacher, Peter, is fantastic! He used to play with the group The Tall Trees.
Jack:	Really? Wow! They were a great band! Is there a class on Friday?
Martin:	I don't know. I go on Tuesdays now, but I have to change to Thursdays next term because I've just passed the Level 5 exams.
Jack:	You must be very good. How often do you practise?
Martin:	Every day! I spend an hour and sometimes two in my room and on Saturday mornings my band spends three hours practising. We're called The Red Chillies!
Jack:	Cool.
Martin:	Actually, we're playing in the town music festival on Saturday. I've got a free ticket. Do you want to come?
Jack:	Yes! Thanks very much. Is it at the music school?
Martin:	No. Last year it was in the music school, but this year it's in the park, near the shopping centre. It's going to be great. Can you bring your camera to take photos?
Jack:	Of course! What time will you be on stage?
Martin:	Well, I need to arrive at quarter past six and there's a singing competition at quarter past seven, but I think we're starting at quarter to eight.
Jack:	OK. We can have dinner in the Street Café afterwards.
Martin:	That sounds great. See you on Saturday!
Jack:	OK. Bye.
Narrator:	Now listen again.

3a

Favourite things	Hobbies	Places to go	Things to do at the weekend
a bike	cooking	the beach	go to a festival
a camera	painting	the cinema	go to a restaurant
a fishing rod	reading	a museum	have a barbecue
a mobile phone	taking photos	the park	have a picnic

3b *Sample answers*

1 I go running and I play computer games.
2 Yes, I can. I can play the piano.
3 My favourite thing is my mobile phone because I can listen to music, take photos and talk to my friends.
4 We usually meet in the café or at the sports centre.
5 I go to the cinema about once a year.
6 I watched a film on tv and played golf with my brother.
7 I'm going to have a barbecue with my friends.
8 Yes, I have. I went to a music festival in July.

Listening Part 3:2

1
1 download	6 digital camera
2 mobile phone	7 online
3 internet	8 keyboards
4 video games	9 mouse
5 web page	10 emails

2 1 A   2 A   3 B   4 B   5 C

Narrator: 🔊 **Track 12 Listening Part 3 Worksheet 2**

Listen to Lisa talking to her friend Robert about computers.
For each question, choose the right answer A, B or C.
You will hear the conversation twice.
Look at questions 1–5 now. You have twenty seconds.
Now listen to the conversation.

Robert: Hi Lisa. How are you?

Lisa: Tired! I went to bed at midnight, so I need a coffee!

Robert: Were you writing text messages to your friends again?

Lisa: No! My sister Paula's written a blog about her trip to Australia. I was reading it. The photos look amazing on my new laptop.

Robert: Really? I need to buy a new computer. Where did you get it?

Lisa: In town. I went to the store on the High Street and I also looked in Green's Computer Store on Park Avenue but they were very expensive, so I bought it in the little shop on Bridge Street.

Robert: How did you choose it?

Lisa: Well, first of all, I looked at some web pages on my phone. There wasn't much information on 'New laptop dot com' but 'Buy a computer dot com' was great.

Robert: If I buy a laptop, I'll have to take it to university with me every day. Is yours heavy?

Lisa: No, it's one and a half kilogrammes, but my old one was three kilogrammes. I carried it in my backpack every day. The best ones these days are only one kilogramme!

Robert: Wow! Was the one you bought expensive?

Lisa: Well, the one I really wanted cost £849!

Robert: Really?

Lisa: Yes, but I didn't get it. The shop assistant also showed me one for £579 but it didn't have a very big memory. I spent £699 in the end.

Robert: Are you going to use it at university too?

Lisa: Yes, that's why I bought it. I'm going to need it for my course next year! But first I'm going to help my brother to improve the website for his camera shop. He's got one, but it's awful!

Robert: Cool! That sounds interesting!

Narrator: Now listen again.

3
1 The first mobile phone was invented in 1973 (by Martin Cooper).
2 Videos are watched on the internet (by lots of people).
3 That email wasn't written by my brother.
4 News articles are often read online (by people).
5 The first website was created in 1991 (by Tim Berners-Lee).
6 Video games are usually played at home (by young people).
7 The students were shown some useful websites (by the teacher).

Listening Part 3:3

1
1 comics	6 diary
2 textbook	7 passport
3 menu	8 postcard
4 magazines	9 ticket
5 newspaper	10 article

2 1 C   2 C   3 A   4 B   5 B

Narrator: 🔊 **Track 13 Listening Part 3 Worksheet 3**

Listen to James talking to Susan about his holiday.

For each question, choose the right answer A, B or C.

You will hear the conversation twice.

Look at questions 1–5 now. You have twenty seconds.

Now listen to the conversation.

Susan: Are you excited about your holiday, James?

James: Yes, I am! Actually, will you feed my cat for me while I'm away?

Susan: Of course, no problem. You fed my fish while I was in Rome.

James: Thanks. His food's in the cupboard under the window and his bowl is on the floor by the door. If I leave the plants on the kitchen table will you water them too?

Susan: Sure. How long are you away for?

James: Three weeks, but some friends are going to stay at my house for two weeks so you'll only need to go there for the final week. I'll be home on the 30th.

Susan: OK. That's good. You haven't told me where you're going yet.

James: To Miami and Paris.

Susan: Wow!

James: Yes, There are flights to France from Manchester every day so I'm spending a few days exploring Paris before I fly to Miami.

Susan: That sounds amazing. Have you ever been to the USA?

James: No, I haven't. I went to Mexico when I was younger and I went skiing in Canada in January, but I've never been to the USA.

Susan: And how long is the flight to Miami?

James: It's eight and a half hours, which is OK, but the return journey will take over sixteen hours because I have to spend five hours waiting in New York!

Susan: That's a long time! Do you want me to meet you at Manchester airport when you get back?

James: That would be great. … Let me check the times on my phone … OK, I arrive at gate one at five thirty five in the afternoon. The flight number's eleven oh five. Shall I email you the information?

Susan: Yes please! And don't forget to send me a postcard while you're away!

James: I won't!

Narrator: Now listen again.

3a 1 f 2 c 3 e 4 i 5 g
       6 d 7 a 8 j 9 h 10 b

3b Students' own answers

Get it right!

This present **was given to me** by my old German friend.

Listening Part 4:1

1a 1 yesterday 4 century 7 birthday
      2 clock 5 diary 8 evening
      3 weekly 6 Autumn

1b

at	In	on	no preposition
half past three the moment the weekend	January the afternoon 2013	Friday morning Mondays 15th May	every day last year tomorrow

2 1 1993 4 31st August
     2 3/three 5 212 456 938
     3 2/two (small) dogs

Narrator: 🔊 **Track 14 Listening Part 4 Worksheet 1**

You will hear a woman talking to a customer about renting a boat.

Listen and complete each question.

You will hear the conversation twice.

Woman: Hello Broads Boat Rentals.

Philip: Hello. I'd like to rent a boat in August please.

Woman: Yes, of course. I need to ask you some questions first. Is that OK?

Philip: Of course.

Woman: First of all, what's your name?

Philip: Philip Cook.

Woman: Philip Cook … right … And what's your date of birth, Philip?

Philip: It's 1st December 1993.

Woman: That's fine. You need to be over 21 to rent a sailing boat. And how many people will be staying on the boat?

Philip: There will be three of us. My brother Tom and I and our friend. We're all over 21. Some other friends might come for the day but they won't sleep on the boat. Is that OK?

Woman: That's fine. And will there be any animals?

Philip: I don't think Lee is going to bring his dog, I have two small dogs.

Woman: That's no problem, but you have to pay extra for every pet. And when would you like to rent the boat?

Philip:	From the 23rd of August to the 31st of August. We wanted to rent it until the 3rd of September but your website says your office closes on the 1st of September!
Woman:	Yes, that's right, I'm afraid. And finally, can you give me your telephone number please?
Philip:	Yes. It's 212 456 938. That's 2-1-2, 4-5-6, 9-3-8.
Woman:	212 456 938. Perfect. Thank you, one of our sailing assistants will call you next week with more information.
Philip:	Thank you. Bye!
Narrator:	Now listen again.

3 1 a   2 a   3 c   4 b   5 c
    6 b   7 c   8 b   9 c   10 a

Listening Part 4:2

1   1 brain   6 neck
    2 tooth   7 fingers
    3 eyes   8 heart
    4 hair   9 stomach
    5 feet   10 hand

2   1 13   4 Spanish
    2 Moore   5 567582
    3 9.00/9/nine am

Narrator:	🔊 **Track 15 Listening Part 4 Worksheet 2**
	You will hear a man telephoning a medical centre for advice. Listen and complete each question. You will hear the conversation twice.
Woman:	Hello, Medical Centre. How can I help you?
Man:	Hi. Yes. My daughter has had an accident and I need some medical advice.
Woman:	OK. Could you tell me what's happened, please?
Man:	We were on the beach and Katrina was jumping in the sea. She fell and has hurt her foot. It isn't broken, but she can't walk.
Woman:	OK. Well, first, she should sit down on the floor and put her foot up on a chair. Then you should go to a chemist and buy a bandage.
Man:	Right. At the moment, we're still near Greenbank Beach. Could you tell me where the nearest chemist is? We don't have a car.

Woman:	There's a big chemist in the city centre but if you are on the beach, the nearest chemist is in Park Street. There's a bus stop nearby, or you can get a taxi there.
Man:	OK. How much will a taxi cost?
Woman:	About 13 euros.
Man:	Great. Thank you for your help.
Woman:	Your daughter should probably come and see a doctor here tomorrow morning. Would you like to make an appointment?
Man:	Oh, yes. That's a good idea.
Woman:	Would you like to come at nine, or half past nine?
Man:	9 o'clock is fine. What's the doctor's name?
Woman:	OK. Tomorrow the 10th of May ... at nine o'clock ... with Doctor Moore. That's M-O-O-R-E. Did you say your daughter's name is Katrina?
Man:	Yes. I'm afraid Katrina doesn't speak a lot of English. Does the doctor speak any Spanish?
Woman:	Yes. She lived in Mexico for ten years, so she speaks it quite well.
Man:	That's fantastic. We will buy a bandage now and come to the centre tomorrow.
Woman:	OK. Katrina shouldn't walk until tomorrow, if possible. If you need any more advice, call the hospital on 56 75 82. That's 5-6 7-5 8-2.
Man:	Thank you very much. See you tomorrow.
Woman:	You're welcome. Goodbye.
Narrator:	Now listen again.

3   1 should   5 should
    2 might; shouldn't   6 shouldn't; might
    3 should   7 should
    4 should   8 shouldn't

Listening Part 4:3

1a   1st first   12th twelfth
     2nd second   13th thirteenth
     3rd third   14th fourteenth
     4th fourth   20th twentieth
     5th fifth   25th twenty-fifth
     9th ninth   31st thirty-first

1b   1 second   7 twenty-fifth
     2 third   8 ninth
     3 fifth   9 fourteenth
     4 twelfth   10 fourth
     5 thirty-first   11 twentieth
     6 thirteenth   12 first

Get it right!

It is very important to me because I am going to New Zealand tomorrow.

2 1 Wednesdays
    2 £75
    3 August
    4 9/nine pm/21.00
    5 Bracknell Street

Narrator: 🔊 **Track 16 Listening Part 4 Worksheet 3**

You will hear a woman talking to a receptionist about photography lessons. Listen and complete each question. You will hear the conversation twice.

Man: Hello, Townhill College. Can I help you?

Woman: Hi, yes. I'd like some information about your photography classes, please.

Man: Well, photography is very popular so there are two courses. They both start on the 3rd of October and finish on the 10th of December.

Woman: OK. And what days of the week are the classes?

Man: Last term they were on Fridays, but this term they are on Wednesdays.

Woman: And how much do they cost?

Man: The morning course costs £50, and the evening course is a bit more expensive. It costs £75.

Woman: OK. And can I join the evening class over the phone?

Man: No, you have to come to the college and fill in a form. We'll be closed in August but are open for the rest of July and will open again in September.

Woman: Are you open at weekends?

Man: No. We're open Monday to Friday from 9.30 am to 12.45 pm and 5.30 pm to 9.00 pm.

Woman: Can you give me the address of the college, please? I'll come and fill in the form next week.

Man: Yes, it's in 59 Bracknell Street. That B-R-A-C-K-N-E-L-L Street. Near the children's playground, opposite the bank.

Woman: Will I need to buy any equipment for the class?

Man: I think you need your own camera, but the teacher will send you an email about the classes at the end of September.

Woman: OK great. What's the teacher's name?

Man: It's Bob. I don't know his surname.

Woman: Thank you very much! I'll come to the college one day next week to pay for the course then.

Man: You're welcome. See you next week.

Narrator: Now listen again.

---

3 1 b   2 c   3 b   4 c
   5 a   6 b   7 c   8 a

Listening Part 5:1

1 1 a   2 a   3 b   4 c   5 a
   6 c   7 b   8 c   9 a   10 c

2 1 three / 3
    2 (his) pets
    3 curtains
    4 book case / book shelf
    5 (some) apple

Narrator: 🔊 **Track 17 Listening Part 5 Worksheet 1**

You will hear a radio programme about a house. Listen and complete each question. You will hear the information twice.

Presenter: Welcome to **Who lives here?**, the radio show which explores famous people's houses. Today we are visiting the footballer Matt Jackson's house, which was built over one hundred years ago. It's got six bedrooms and three bathrooms. Matt's family must be very fit because this house has got three floors! At the moment, I'm standing in the hall and I can see lots of photographs. Most of them are of Matt's children but there are some photos of his pets too. OK, let's go into the living room, Matt's favourite room. Wow! It's a beautiful space, with a dark green carpet and long, green curtains at the windows. There's a comfortable brown sofa and a lamp near the window. There's an old, wooden bookshelf too. If I look out of the window, I can see the garden. Matt's family must enjoy spending time there! It's full of colourful flowers and he's got some apple trees and a swimming pool too … (fading out) … at the end of the garden …

Narrator: Now listen again.

3
1 Do you live in a flat or a house/in a house or a flat?
2 How many bedrooms has it got?
3 What colour is your front door?
4 Have you got a garden?
5 Where do you usually watch TV?
6 Have you got an armchair in your bedroom?
7 Is there a clock in your living room?
8 Do you live in a city?

Students' own answers.

Listening Part 5:2

1a
1 4739841	4 2375881
2 6639824	5 3654298
3 95344387	

Narrator: 🔊 **Track 18 Listening Part 5 Worksheet 2**

Listen and write the phone numbers.

Narrator: **One**

Boy 1: Hi Tom, what's your phone number?

Boy 2: It's four seven three, nine eight four one.

Narrator: **Two**

Woman: If you want more information, please call Lesley on six six three, nine eight two four.

Narrator: **Three**

Man: Peter, can you call the Elliot Hotel, please? The number is nine five three, double four three eight seven.

Narrator: **Four**

Woman: Is this the doctor's number, here on the fridge? Two three seven, five double-eight one?

Man: Yes, that's right.

Narrator: **Five**

Man: Hello. Could you give me the number of the Chinese restaurant on Melton Street, please?

Woman: Yes, of course. Three six five, four two nine eight.

1b
1 seven two three nine eight five three
2 eight nine four one nine one two
3 four nine two one three five eight
4 four seven six nine three three five
5 six seven four six eight two nine

2
1 10/ten	4 online
2 (Red House) café	5 654397831
3 August	

Narrator: 🔊 **Track 19 Listening Part 5 Worksheet 2**

You will hear a woman talking about a music festival.
Listen and complete each question.
You will hear the information twice.

Woman: Hello everyone! Don't forget that this Saturday we're having the second City Music Day on Bridge Street. Come along and join in the fun! The festival starts at half past ten and there will be free activities for children aged 6 to 10 all day. For example, there will be a singing competition in the Red House Café at 11.45 am – the first prize is a ticket to the Summer Stars Festival in August. In the afternoon Jim Saunders will be playing the guitar at the town hall. Buy your tickets for his show now online, but be quick! Last year his concert was very popular and this year there are only a hundred tickets for sale. For more information about any of the activities call Jacky Webb on 654 397 831, that's six five four, three nine seven, eight three one. We look forward to seeing you on Saturday. Remember, the fun starts at ten thirty!

Narrator: Now listen again.

3
1 Call; b	6 Send; j
2 Phone; a	7 fill in; d
3 Look; f	8 Ask; h
4 Don't talk; i	9 go; c
5 show; e	10 Meet; g

Listening Part 5:3

1
1 must	5 have
2 mustn't	6 don't
3 must	7 have
4 not	8 to

2
1 8.30/eight thirty
2 The (school) secretary
3 painting
4 (Mobile) phones
5 (in the) park

Narrator: **Track 20 Listening Part 5 Worksheet 3**

You will hear a teacher talking about a school trip.
Listen and complete each question.
You will hear the information twice.

Teacher: OK. Everyone, I'm going to tell you some important things about our visit to the City Art Gallery tomorrow. First of all, you don't have to wear your school uniform, but please do wear comfortable shoes. The bus will leave the school at 9.00 am, so you must arrive at half past eight. If you are going to be late, telephone the school secretary. You can also meet the class at the museum at 10.00 am. We will meet a tour guide in the museum at half past ten. He knows a lot about all of the paintings, but tomorrow he will show us the five most important pictures in the gallery. You must listen carefully because you will have to write about your favourite painting for homework. You mustn't use cameras or mobile phones inside the museum, but you can write things down, so bring a notebook and a pen. Finally, remember that you have to bring some food and drink because there isn't a café in the museum. We will eat our lunch in the park after our visit. Are there any questions?

Narrator: Now listen again.

3a 1 You have to eat lots of fruit and vegetables.
2 You mustn't run in the corridors!
3 You need to take this medicine for ten days.
4 You don't have to help me.
5 You must turn off your mobile phone in an exam.
6 You needn't shout, I can hear you!

3b 1 has 4 needn't
2 mustn't 5 doesn't have
3 must 6 need

Get it right!
You have to bring a book and a pencil case.

Speaking Part 1:1

1 1 e 2 h 3 d 4 c 5 g 6 f

2 1 What's your name?
2 And what's your surname?
3 How do you spell that?
4 Where are you from?

5 Who is your English teacher?
6 When did you start learning English?
7 What time do you get up in the morning?
8 Have you got any brothers or sisters?
9 How often do you listen to music?
10 Do you like reading books?
11 Tell me something about your best friend.
12 Tell me something about your favourite TV programme.

3 1 surname 6 daughter
2 wife 7 teenagers
3 brothers 8 cousins
4 aunt 9 neighbours
5 grandfather 10 parents

Speaking Part 1:2

1 1 evening 6 quarter
2 o'clock 7 afternoon
3 tomorrow 8 past
4 Tuesday 9 week
5 meeting 10 morning

2 1 What's your name?
2 And what's your surname?
3 How do you spell that/it?
4 Who cooks/makes/eats dinner in/at your house?
5 What time do you get up?
6 Where do you usually eat/have lunch?
7 What do you wear at the weekend?
8 When do you meet your friends?
9 Where do you do your English homework?
10 Do you like playing computer games?
11 Tell me something about last weekend.
12 Tell me something about your favourite sport.

3 1 I never get up early at the weekend.
2 My brother always reads comics.
3 We often eat pizza on Saturdays.
4 It is usually sunny in the summer.
5 I always have English classes on Mondays.
6 I am sometimes tired in the evenings.
7 I usually leave the house at half past eight.
8 My dad sometimes rides a motorbike to work.
9 I never do the cooking at home.
10 I often meet my friends in the evening.

Speaking Part 1:3

1 1 c 2 b 3 b 4 c 5 a
6 a 7 a 8 b 9 b 10 c

2 1 your 7 many
2 what's 8 go
3 spell 9 How
4 Where 10 your/the
5 do 11 about
6 there 12 Tell me

3 1 h 2 f 3 a 4 g
  5 d 6 c 7 b 8 e

Get it right!
What time **can you** come?

Key Speaking Part 2:1

1 1 d 2 h 3 e 4 c
  5 f 6 a 7 b 8 g

2 *Suggested answers*
Appleton Castle
Where is the castle? On Treetop Hill.
What can I see? A beautiful garden and a museum
Is it open on Sunday? No, it isn't.
How much is a student's ticket? £5
Can I buy food? Yes, you can buy sandwiches
and drinks.

Painting lessons
When does the class start? On the 11th January
Are the classes big? No, they aren't. They are small.
How much do the classes cost? £25
Who is the teacher? Her name is Joanna Jackson.
What is the telephone number? 245932

3 1 August   6 July
  2 autumn   7 September
  3 December   8 spring
  4 February   9 summer
  5 January   10 winter

Key Speaking Part 2:2

1 1 throw   6 watch
  2 ride   7 cycle
  3 hit   8 kick
  4 practise   9 win
  5 swim   10 go

2 *Suggested answers*
Tennis lessons
Where are the tennis lessons? They are in City Park.
How can I find more information? You can find out
  more at www.playtennis.com.
Does the advanced class start at 6:15? No, the
  advanced class starts at 7:45.
Are there classes every day? No, the classes are on
  Tuesday and Thursday.
How much do the lessons cost? They cost £28.50
  every month.

Surfing competition
When does the competition start? It starts at 2 pm.
Where is the competition? The competition is on
  South Beach in front of the café.
Is the competition only for adults? No, all ages
  are welcome.

How much does it cost to enter? It costs £5 and
  the price includes a t-shirt.
What can I win? You can win a digital camera.

3a 1 Where is the sports club? In Blackstone Park
  2 Can I go in June? No. The classes are from
    1st July to 31st August.
  3 Are there lessons on Fridays? Yes. There are
    lessons every day from Monday- Friday.
  4 How can I find more information? You can call
    Peter on 7532456.
  5 How much do the lessons cost? £10 for
    two hours.
  6 Who can go to the sports club? Everyone who
    loves sport.

Key Speaking Part 2:3

1a

A thing	A person	A way to travel	A verb
bridge	driver	bus	catch
bus stop	passenger	car	drive
roundabout	tourist	helicopter	travel
traffic light	visitor	taxi	visit

1b 1 boat   4 bus stop
  2 helicopter   5 traffic light
  3 travel   6 drive

2 *Suggested answers*
Best Buys Travel agents
Are the travel agents open on Saturday?
  Yes. They're open from 9:30 to 1pm on Saturday.
Are the holidays expensive?
  No, they've got cheap holidays (for you and
  your family).
Where are the travel agents?
  The travel agents are in Summerfield Street in Hillford.
Can I go to the USA?
  Yes, they have holidays in/to the USA.
What is the phone number? It's 6-7-8-5-4-3-0

Day trip
Is there a guided tour?
  Yes, there's a tour of the old town with a local guide.
When can I go?
  Every Saturday.
What can I do?
  You can explore the castle and shop in the
local market.
How much does the day trip cost?
  It costs £35, including the train tickets and
  guided tour.
Where can I eat?
  You can have lunch at Fin's fish restaurant.

3 1 c   2 b   3 b   4 c   5 b
  6 c   7 a   8 a   9 c

Get it right!
Write me a letter to tell me what **you are** going to do.

Think about it

Reading and Writing Part 1

1 True
2 False
3 False
4 True
5 True
6 True
7 False
8 True

Reading and Writing Part 2

1 five
2 All
3 a word
4 Under
5 the correct letter
6 are all
7 vocabulary
8 easier

Reading and Writing Part 3

1 five
2 three
3 one
4 two
5 five
6 eight
7 five
8 one

Reading and Writing Part 4

1 reading
2 always
3 a few
4 but you won't
5 (A, B and C)
6 short
7 not given
8 name

Reading and Writing Part 5

1 False
2 False
3 True
4 False
5 True
6 False
7 True
8 True

Reading and Writing Part 6

1 spelling
2 sentences
3 dictionary
4 first
5 line
6 verbs
7 group
8 list

Reading and Writing Part 7

1 read
2 fill
3 answer
4 show
5 choose
6 think
7 write
8 spell

Reading and Writing Part 8

1 posters
2 diary
3 days
4 price
5 spelling
6 answers
7 three
8 one

Reading and Writing Part 9

1 c   2 a   3 d   4 b   5 e

Listening Part 1

1 d
2 e
3 c
4 b
5 a
6 g
7 f
8 h

Listening Part 2

1 simple
2 two
3 activities
4 daily
5 twice
6 five
7 eight
8 question
9 end
10 answer

Listening Part 3

1 choosing A, B or C
2 one long
3 two
4 five
5 know
6 something they are interested in
7 one
8 one point

Listening Part 4

1 True
2 False. The speakers may have Irish, Australian or American accents too.
3 True
4 False. You need to write complete words.
5 False. It might be more than one word.
6 True. But you need to spell simple words correctly.
7 True
8 True

Listening Part 5

1 five
2 one
3 a date, a time or a name (for example)
4 maybe/they might
5 one or more
6 on the question paper.

Speaking Part 1

1 no
2 surname
3 yourself
4 examiner
5 two
6 five to six

Speaking Part 2

1 b   2 e   3 c   4 a   5 d   6 f

ACKNOWLEDGEMENTS

Development of this publication has made use of the Cambridge English Corpus, a multi-billion word collection of spoken and written English. It includes the Cambridge Learner Corpus, a unique collection of candidate exam answers. Cambridge University Press has built up the Cambridge English Corpus to provide evidence about language use that helps to produce better language teaching materials.

The authors and publishers acknowledge the following sources of copyright material and are grateful for the permissions granted. While every effort has been made, it has not always been possible to identify the sources of all the material used, or to trace all copyright holders. If any omissions are brought to our notice, we will be happy to include the appropriate acknowledgements on reprinting and in the next update to the digital edition, as applicable.

p. 6: Wavebreakmedia Ltd/Getty Images; p. 9: Glowimages/Getty Images; p. 12: Michael Krasowitz/Photographer's Choice/Getty Images; p. 14: Verdina Anna/Moment/Getty Images; p. 17: Janine Lamontagne/E+/Getty Images; p. 19: Jamie Grill/Iconica/Getty Images; p. 21: jeffbergen/E+/Getty Images; p. 23: Johnny Louis/Wirelmage/Getty Images; p. 25: Martyn Ferry/Moment/Getty Images; p. 26: Caiaimage/Chris Ryan/OJO+/Getty Images; p. 28: Peter Durant/Passage/Getty Images; p. 30: Jupiterimages/Stockbyte/Getty Images; p. 32: 8213erika/iStock/Getty Images; p. 34: Kenny Bengtsson/Folio/Getty Images; p. 36: A L Christensen/Moment Open/Getty Images; p. 38: Riitta Supperi/Folio Images/Getty Images; p. 40: Sam Edwards/Caiaimage/Getty Images; p. 42: Andersen Ross/DigitalVision/Getty Images; p. 45: Erik Isakson/Getty Images; p. 46: Geri Lavrov/Moment Open/Getty Images; p. 48: John Lund/Paula Zacharias/Blend Images/Getty Images; p. 50: blue jean images/Getty Images; p. 53: ClaudioVentrella/iStock/Getty Images; p. 55: BraunS/E+/Getty Images; p. 56: Steve Debenport/E+/Getty Images; p. 59: John Eder/Stone/Getty Images; p. 66: Jovanmandic/iStock/Getty Images; p. 68: Don Mason/Blend Images/Getty Images; p. 70: Colin Hawkins/Cultura/Getty Images; p. 72: Howard Kingsnorth/Cultura Exclusive/Getty Images; p. 74: monkeybusinessimages/iStock/Getty Images; p. 76: m-imagephotography/iStock/Getty Images; p. 79: Marco Simoni/robertharding/Getty Images; p. 80: Martin Barraud/OJO Images/Getty Images; p. 83: PeopleImages.com/DigitalVision/Getty Images; p. 84: Spaces Images/Blend Images/Getty Images; p. 87: Tim Mosenfelder/Getty Images Entertainment/Getty Images; p. 88: Robert Nickelsberg/Getty Images News/Getty Images; p. 90: Image Source/Getty Images; p. 92: i love images/Cultura/Getty Images; p. 94: Diane Auckland/Passage/Getty Images.

Illustrations by Nigel Dobbyn

The publishers are grateful to the following contributors:
layout by Q2A Media Services Pvt. Ltd.; audio production by Hart McLeod, Cambridge